Writing in the House of Dreams

Reviews

A cracking read… astounding! The dream journey is insightful and dramatic and leads beautifully into the writing exercises.

Lesley Howarth, award-winning author

Jenny carefully weaves the threads of her own life in Shetland and in Cornwall with her knowledge of psychology, anthropology, myths and therapy, and builds a fascinating book for dreamers and for writers.

Penny Dolan, Awfully Big Reviews

It is so smart and so refreshingly original. You don't know where the journey is going to take you or what is coming next. I love that!

Sian Morgan, author and psychologist

I love the ideas to get the writing flowing, and also techniques for capturing dreams (I've had some very interesting ones since starting work on this!)

Helen Greathead, editor

It's very exciting that the extraordinarily beautiful, creative and individual ideas Jenny has shared for years in dream workshops and conversations with friends have finally got a chance to be shared with the world at large.

Liz Kessler, New Your Times bestselling author

This is an astonishing book. I don't think I've read another like it. It's a book of writing exercises and advice on how to write – but, equally, exercises and advice on how to live another life, in your dreams.

Susan Price, award-winning author

How lovely - the idea of enjoying dreams for what they are, without the need for instant interpretation - just a gradual opening to deeper understanding, and how our inner life can enrich both writing, and day to day existence… I was surprised at how quickly my dream recall came back to me after a long gap from recording my dreams.

Josephine Gabriel, writer and blogger

An unusual blend of autobiography, psychology and insights into the creative process centring around the gifts offered by our dreams. I found it fascinating and informative from beginning to end.

Victoria Field, writer and poetry therapist

WRITING IN THE HOUSE OF DREAMS

UNLOCK THE POWER OF YOUR UNCONSCIOUS MIND

JENNY ALEXANDER

five
lanes

Published by Five Lanes Press 2017
Contact info@fivelanespress.co.uk

Previously published as *Writing in the House of Dreams: Creative Adventures for Dreamers and Writers* in 2014.

ISBN: 978-1-910300-16-9 (Paperback)
978-1-910300-17-6 (eBook)

Cover design by Rachel Lawson http://www.lawstondesign.com
Design and typesetting: Zebedee Design

Contents

Introduction

The psyche can be compared to a house, in which most of us inhabit the attic, leaving the rest of the building unexplored. Accordingly, our lives are more constrained than they need to be and much of our capacity lies fallow and unused. From time to time, we may feel that we could make more of our lives, attributing our failure to external circumstances – lack of money or opportunity – not realizing that the necessary resources are available in ourselves. Dreams, if we follow them, lead down to the ground floor and the basement, as well as to the landscape beyond. We might not always like what we find there but, once the exploration is embarked upon, adventures, discoveries and surprises quickly follow.

Anthony Stevens

When you tell acquaintances and strangers that you write and teach about dreams an interesting thing happens – the polite, interested look disappears, their faces light up and they straight away tell you about a dream they've had.

If you're at a party or in a pub, other people will often join in. One person might say he's had a dream about a flying dog and before you know it half a dozen others will get into a discussion about their favourite techniques for dream flying. Do you glide, float, flap or soar? How do you get lift-off?

The same thing happens with writers, when you ask them what they're writing about. Pleasant, sociable chatter turns to passionate engagement as they talk about their characters' problems and dilemmas just as if they were real people in real situations, but with lives much more exciting than real life because in imagination everything is possible.

Real life in this busy, secular, materialistic world can feel flat and vaguely unsatisfying. We may be haunted by a nagging sense that there must be something more... because there is. Beneath the surface of every life, barely explored or even acknowledged, there's fathomless inner world of imagination, or 'House of Dreams'.

Writers and dreamers learn how to come and go easily between the outer and inner worlds. They develop the personal qualities they need in order to enter the House of Dreams, such as patience, curiosity and courage, and acquire skills and techniques such as dream-incubation or interpretation, strong narrative voice or plot-creation that will help them make the best of the treasures they find there.

This coming and going between worlds has a transformative effect. It makes ordinary life feel bigger, better, more exciting, by expanding our experience of ourselves and our lives. The ordinary world is just the melody; the inner world brings in layer upon layer of wonderful harmonies.

And it doesn't stop at coming and going across the border. Because imagination is boundless, this exploration, once embarked upon, can keep taking you deeper and wider, bringing ever more 'adventures, discoveries and surprises'.

I was a dreamer long before I was a writer, so when I came to writing I was already a seasoned traveller in my inner world. As I got to know other writers, I discovered that many of them had complications around the writing process that I didn't, and I devised a programme of writing workshops based on the concepts, attitudes and exercises I had developed through dream-working.

If you are a writer interested in dreams, you will find here a guide to the dream-world and a toolkit of techniques that you will need to explore it, such as how to recall and record your dreams, how to incubate a dream and how to tackle nightmares.

You will also find, as well as practical tips on the writer's craft, different ways of thinking about writing, which will help get rid of any blocks and difficulties, such as being too self-critical, not knowing what to write about or worrying that you might not meet your deadlines.

If you are a dreamer, you will find ideas and exercises that will help you to engage with your dreams creatively as well as interpretatively, through writing. Letting go of the interpretative intention breaks the link between the dream and waking life and opens the way to a more shamanic experience of dreaming.

If you are just someone who enjoys a good story, this book is the story of the greatest adventure of my life.

Each chapter consists of a brief introduction to a new stage in the dreamer's journey, a section of memoir to illustrate it from my own experience, and a practical creative exercise from my writing-and-dreaming workshops designed to help you explore the same ideas through creative writing.

It begins with the loss of the secret magical world of childhood, as we gradually understand what is 'real' and what is 'not real', and learn to live in the ordinary world that everyone knows and shares.

The Ordinary World

There's a great power of imagination about these little creatures, and a creative fancy and belief that is very curious to watch.

William Makepeace Thackeray

One of the great pleasures of spending time with young children is that 'these little creatures' are so different from ourselves. They live in another world because they see things in a completely different way, and the way they see things isn't something they have learned from us; it's their own natural substance.

We are not born a clean slate on which the ability to think and understand things rationally is gradually written. Our lives and personalities are not built, block by block, on worldly experience alone.

Babies in the womb display all the physical signs of dreaming, and so it seems that the dream is there first, before mother and father, family, culture. We are born out of the dream and emerge, still cocooned, into the magical world of childhood, where teddies can talk, fairies grant wishes and monsters hide in the shadows.

As long as we are young enough to feel protected by the magical power of our parents, and by our own magical powers, we can stay in that shape-shifting world, but we soon become aware that in the grown-up world the magic doesn't work.

Then we want and need to leave the dream and learn to think like an adult, to understand the rules of the ordinary world that everybody shares, so that we can survive and thrive in it.

> **I was lying in a shallow ditch. I had no idea how I had got there. The earth underneath me felt warm and grainy, and the sun on my bare arms and legs made my skin tingle...**

Life is resonant. Small events set up vibrations in the soul which still reverberate long after the event itself is forgotten. So it was with the ants on a hot summer day in 1955 which, two years later, were to bring me my first understanding of dreams.

I was making mud pies on the back step, scraping the dry earth into my bucket, adding water from the dribbling outdoor tap and stirring the mixture like my mother did when she made fairy cakes for tea. I spooned it out in sloppy dollops onto the hot concrete and, by the time I had found enough small stones for cherries, my mud pies were already drying out, going hard and pale at the edges.

My mother was at the kitchen sink doing the washing. The hankies were boiling on the stove and she had the back door open to let the steam out. My father was mowing the grass. I could hear the whirr-whirr of the blades behind me as he pushed the mower up and down. My big sister Susan was riding her bike, bumping and rattling along the path that ran down the side of the garden to the wooden gate at the bottom.

Our garden was a large patch of scrubby grass, featureless except for a washing-line and a compost heap in the far corner comprised entirely of grass cuttings. On one side, a chain-link fence separated the garden from next door's identical one, and then another chain-link fence, and another, all the way to the main road. On the other side, a tall hedge hid the flower beds and orchards that surrounded the big bungalow at the end of the close.

We heard Monica calling but we couldn't see her over the hedge. Susan ran down to the gate. I ran after her. I always followed although Susan never asked me to and sometimes I ended up wishing I hadn't. I hoped Monica wouldn't have her doctor's set with her because, if she did, they would make me be the patient. They would take me to secret places and hold me down. Susan would wield the syringe, of course – she was the expert when it came to injections.

We went out of the gate and clambered over the stile into the woods, where Monica was waiting impatiently.

'I've found something!' she said to Susan. 'Come and see.'

I followed them along the dirt path under the trees. Monica was pulling a plank of wood along the ground behind her, tied to a piece of string. I didn't know what it was for, and I didn't like not knowing. Suddenly, Monica stopped.

There was a dead animal lying under the long grass at the side of the path. It had a dribble of dried blood stuck to its face where its eye should be.

'What is it?' Susan said.

'I don't know,' said Monica. 'But we're going to pick it up and put it on my sledge.'

They both looked at me.

I was frightened of Monica. She wasn't as big as Susan, but she had bright ginger hair, and her pale face was covered in freckles. She claimed she could eat the skin of oranges, and I had seen her mother do it, her bright red lipstick lips drawn back from her teeth. When I tried to do it myself, I couldn't. Even the fleshy pith was too bitter.

I looked at the animal. I didn't ask why we had to put it on the plank, or where we were going to take it. There were fat flies buzzing around it and ants crawling in and out of its fur. I wanted to run back along the path, but I couldn't see the house from there and I wasn't sure of the way.

My sister flicked at the flies with a bit of bracken.

'Go on then,' she said.

Monica put her hand on her hip, her orange hair gleaming dangerously. Susan's hair was black, in thick curls around her face. They were both much bigger than me. I could feel the ants crawling in the rat's wiry fur as I picked it up.

No one knew about the rat, but here's a photo
our mother took at the seaside of me holding
another dead animal that Susan and Monica found

The ants crawled out of the rat and surfaced again soon after when I was watching a film on television with my father. The Indians buried the cowboys up to their necks and smeared honey on their faces.

'Why have they given them honey?' I asked my dad. 'Is it to tease them because they can't reach to lick it up?'

Before he could answer, the ants came and everything became horribly clear.

So the ants crawled out of the rat bringing fear and revulsion, and they came to the honey, and they hurt the cowboys, and then, with fear and revulsion and cruelty, they marched on. They caught up with me two years later, when my family had moved to a suburban street far, far away from the woods.

I was lying in a shallow ditch. I had no idea how I had got there. The earth underneath me felt warm and grainy, and the sun on my bare arms and legs made my skin tingle. I raised my head and looked down at my body. There was an ant on my leg. I stiffened. Suddenly, the ants were everywhere. I wanted to brush them off but I found I couldn't move. I started to scream.

My mother came rushing into the bedroom.

'Get them off me!' I shouted. 'Make them go away!'

'What? Get what off you? What's the matter?'

I couldn't tell whether my mother was angry or scared, like me.

'The ants! Get them off me!'

My mother said, 'There aren't any ants here. You must have been having a dream.'

What did she mean, there weren't any ants? I could see them. I could feel them crawling all over me. I started to scream again.

15

My mother ran out and came back with my dad. He stood in the doorway in his pyjamas, bleary with sleep.

'Get them off me!' I yelled.

The ants were everywhere. They were nibbling at my skin. They were eating right through to my bones.

'What's going on?' my father asked, talking to my mother, not me.

'Just tell her there aren't any ants.'

He nodded, and pulled back the blankets. He said, 'Look, Jennifer. No ants. There aren't any ants.'

I couldn't see them now, but I knew what I had seen, and I knew what I had felt. I knew what every five-year-old knows – that dreams are real. The only difference between the ants on the rat and the ants in the ditch was that nobody else could see the ants in the ditch. In dreams, you were on your own.

After my mother and father had gone back to bed, I lay there rigid, not daring to move in case the ants came back. Then I did what every child eventually does – I turned my face away from the dream towards the light streaming in from the landing.

I looked away and my dreams disappeared, as dreams will.

> I learned that you should feel when writing, not like Lord Byron on a mountain top, but like a child stringing beads in kindergarten, happy, absorbed and quietly putting one bead on after another.
>
> Brenda Ueland

We have to leave the magical world of childhood to live in the ordinary world but it remains our root and essence. Carl Jung said that the dream goes on all the time beneath the surface throughout life, although we only experience it in sleep when the distractions of the dayworld are silenced. James Hillman described it as part of the human psyche, the 'imaginal layer' – where reason holds no sway and imagination rules.

We can't live in it wholly, like young children, but we can reconnect with it once we have fully understood and rooted ourselves in the reality of waking life. The key to reconnecting with the 'imaginal layer' of our self through dreams and creative activities is the ability to put our pragmatic, logical, adult way of understanding on hold and think like a child.

The child mind is characterised by curiosity, playfulness, openness and non-judgement; it is infused with a sense of wonder. To engage with dreams in our child mind we need to put aside all thoughts of interpretation, and not allow ourselves to run ahead looking for rational explanations even before we decide which dreams are worth recording, as our adult mind is inclined to do.

To engage with creative work of any kind we need to keep the adult, critical voice out of the way, and allow our inner child to delight in the simple joy of finding out what the story or picture or song wants to be.

Dorothea Brande expresses this brilliantly in her book, *Becoming a Writer*, which was first published in 1934 and is still in print today (that tells you how good it is). She suggests that writers should think of themselves as two people – the spontaneous child and the adult, the artist and the critic – or as a person with two minds, the unconscious and the intellect.

These two people, these two minds, are both essential in becoming a writer, and we need to train them both in their particular skills but keep them apart, not letting the critical intellect interfere before the work of the unconscious is finished but also not letting the unconscious refuse to hand over to the critical process when its work is done.

There are two stages to every piece of writing, and the first is the realm of the spontaneous child. The joy of the first draft is that it doesn't have to be good because you will be redrafting. All you need from your first draft is to find a structure that works and a voice.

The second stage belongs to the critical mind, which shapes, sorts and selects. It decides what is good and tries to make it better. It works on language and style. It doesn't stop until the story is the best it can possibly be.

In my writing workshops I concentrate more on the first stage because I find that's nearly always where people are stuck. They might have been stuck there since school, wanting to write and not being able to get started, or they might have got stuck in the middle of their novel.

Whenever writing gets stuck and for whatever apparent reason – a failure of confidence, a lack of ideas, a problem with structure – it's almost invariably because the writer has run ahead and allowed the critic, or adult mind to interfere too soon.

I think that's the function of writer's block – it forces you to stop trying to take control and start listening again with the open, adventurous mind of a child. Feeling blocked isn't a problem, but part of the creative process.

Carl Jung said that creativity isn't a product of the intellect but rather of the play instinct, and Brenda Ueland captures this idea when she says that when we write we should feel like a child in kindergarten, happily stringing beads.

Writing about your childhood can be a powerful way of remembering how it felt to be in your child mind and that's why, in my writing courses, I teach sessions on autobiography and memoir including one I call Seed Stories.

I had forgotten about the rat on the plank and the ants in the ditch until, somewhere along my writing journey, I came across the idea that three random incidents you remember from your childhood can contain the seeds of all your stories in later life.

They have to be private memories, things no one has ever talked about, so you can be certain they are authentically yours. They can't be the sort of anecdotes people in the family remember and share, because those have a kind of group ownership.

No one in our family except Susan and me knew about the rat, and by the time I remembered it she was long dead. If our parents had known, I'm sure they would not have thought it significant. The same thing goes for my dream about the ants and my third story, which was about the day the vicar came.

Once I had written my three Seed Stories I began to see they do indeed contain the earliest beginnings of several important themes in my life – dreams, death and God. These threads have run through everything: they are both the motivation and the substance of this book.

Here is the exercise, in case you'd like to try it yourself.

Seed Stories

You'll need a pen and paper, a quiet place, about an hour of free time and an open, receptive frame of mind.

Warm-ups

a) Begin with a warm-up to get the memories flowing. First write some headings down one side of the paper:

Favourite foods at home
Best and worst school dinners
Favourite toys
Favourite items of clothing
Pets
Holidays/outings
People I liked/admired
People I disliked/ feared
Favourite books
Favourite radio/ TV/ films
Family catch-phrases/ songs

Then jot down the first random things that come into your head for each one, not selecting or censoring. These are notes, just words and phrases, not long-winded descriptions. They can be from any stage of your childhood before the age of about ten, in no particular order. Take ten minutes. Enjoy it!

b) The second warm-up is to move into writing mode with a few short timed pieces.

The idea here is that you write for two minutes continuously, keeping your pen moving on the paper, the first things that come into your head on a theme. The reason they're so short is because then you don't have time to ponder and select or, to put it another way, your inner critic can't get a look in.

The timed writing warm-ups in the Seed Stories session are descriptions of childhood places, so choose two or three from this list:

My mother's kitchen
My classroom
My favourite place to play
My grandparents' garden
My childhood bedroom.

This is choosing with your playful mind, not with your intellect, so don't think about which ones will be most appropriate and telling, just which ones you fancy writing about right now. Use all your senses – that's the key to vivid remembering just as it's the key to effective scene-setting in fiction.

Stories

Now that you're in the zone, forget about your warm-ups and write a list of the first random, non-momentous incidents that come to mind from your pre-teen years. Avoid the big familiar stories that have become part of your family's shared history and the ones you have thought about a lot and feel are significant.

Choose three to write about, the first ones that call to you, not worrying about whether they are the best ones. Let yourself be surprised. Spend a maximum of ten minutes on each of them. That's long enough for a first draft, which is basically just about finding the story. You can redraft it later if you want to.

If you enjoy writing seed stories, there's no need to stop at three. Every authentic childhood memory, vividly recalled, reconnects you with your creative centre in the open, emotional, wondering mind of the child.

> **Our normal waking consciousness, rational consciousness as we call it, is but one special type of consciousness, whilst all about it, parted from it by the filmiest of screens, there lie potential forms of consciousness entirely different.**
>
> **William James**

The ordinary world of work and relationships, money and shopping, sports and activities is like the surface of a pond; underneath is the inner life, teeming with stories, themes and images that drive and energise the world above. We are born out of it and return to it every night in sleep, although we may be barely more aware of it than we are of our own heartbeat.

Recalling and recording dreams is the supreme way of

breaking into the inner world, capturing its bright contents and letting them bring colour, depth and meaning to the ordinary world. Writing will do the same thing, and I think that's one hidden reason why so many people want to write.

Because the first stage of writing is so like dreaming, a lot of the quotations I used in my early writing workshops actually came from books about dreaming and one day somebody asked me if I taught workshops on dreams.

I called my first series of dream workshops 'Opening to Dreams' and I had an exciting plan, but I lost my nerve and jettisoned it after the first session because I felt people had come with the assumption that the workshops would be about dream interpretation and, being a bit of a pleaser, I wanted to deliver.

I had been to lots of workshops about dreams as well as working in different interpretative traditions with various experts, and finding meaning had been a regular aspect of my dreaming life for several decades, so I didn't feel unequal to the task; I just felt disappointed.

What I wanted my workshop participants to experience was the excitement of entering the world of imagination like a child, experiencing it directly in all its power, not filtered through ideas and explanations, which are the tools of the ordinary world.

So after that I didn't try to teach dreaming on its own, but along with writing, calling my workshops 'Writing in the House of Dreams', to make it clear from the outset that their primary purpose was creative rather than interpretative.

Dream awareness and writing are both ways of breaking out from our 'rational consciousness' and experiencing 'forms of consciousness entirely different.' A life lived too much on the surface may be haunted by a sense of something missing or lost, forgotten or unrealised, and that's when we may hear the call to dreams.

Part One

Crossing the Threshold

This part is about letting go of the traditional western interpretative approach to dreaming and engaging with dreams as a creative resource.

1 The Call to Dreams

The link can be made between creative living and life itself, and the reasons can be studied why it is that creative living can be lost and why the individual's feeling that life is real or meaningful can disappear.

DW Winnicott

The call to dreams often comes from a vague sense of dissatisfaction, a feeling that 'there must be more to life than this.' It comes from a yearning for meaning, excitement and colour in a world which can feel humdrum, boring and bland.

But it can be a difficult call to answer. Hearing it will often lead to false starts and excuses. Even people who have taken the first step and signed up for workshops because they really want to explore their dreams can get last-minute jitters and look around for sensible reasons not to.

They may say, 'I don't actually have many dreams', or 'I'll never be able to remember them'. They may protest they're in too much of a rush in the morning to commit to writing anything down.

They will sometimes express doubts about the point of remembering dreams, when they're no more than a waste-disposal system for processing the experiences of the day/ don't mean anything/ are impossible to understand.

A few people worry that recalling dreams is going against nature – the unconscious must be unconscious for a reason. But I say dreaming is like meditation. That isn't natural either. It doesn't just happen. It takes dedication and practice, but people who practise it find it beneficial physically, emotionally and in terms of consciousness.

I ask them to put their ideas and theories about what dreams are on one side, because dreaming isn't something you can understand in a theoretical way; you can only understand it through experience.

Even experienced dreamers who usually remember several dreams a week can suddenly hit a dry patch in the run-up to starting a course, because they're unnerved by taking the adventure further and when we begin the second series of workshops, going into the landscape beyond, some will stop recalling for a week or two, before engaging at the next level.

The call to creative writing comes from a similar place and like the call to dreams it can be hard to answer. People who come to writing workshops often start with reservations and resistance. They say they won't be able to write anything good because they were no good at English at school/ they don't understand about grammar/ there are too many books out there already, so what's the point?

Most commonly, they say they haven't got time to write. They're either too busy or they feel guilty about spending what little free time they have on self-indulgent pleasures. But these are just excuses.

Most authors, when they start out, have to fit their writing around their day job or other commitments. They have to get up at five and write before work, or burn the midnight oil after the family have gone to bed. I wrote my first batch of books in two hours a day, while my youngest child was at playgroup.

If you really want to make space in your life for writing or dreaming, you will, but you may first have to overcome some resistance. The refusal of the call is natural, because the adventure is frightening.

In *The Art of Dreaming* by Carlos Castaneda, Don Juan tells the narrator that he should regard dreaming as something extremely dangerous, right from the outset. The author EL Doctorow says that writers are not just people who sit down and write. They put themselves at risk because 'every time you compose a book your composition of yourself is at stake'.

There is genuine risk in embarking upon this road of dreaming and writing. You are going into the unknown, the un-conscious. You will make discoveries which will change how you see yourself and the world and therefore it is appropriate to feel afraid, because you have everything to lose.

But that loss is precisely the opportunity the call to dreams presents, the chance to shed your old ideas like a snake shedding its skin; to be less constrained by what you think you are and what the world is, to let go of what you think you should be, and move more completely into yourself.

The call may be quiet if your waking life is working reasonably well. It may be a single arresting image that intrigues you, or a dream that repeats many times, so you feel it is trying to tell you something. It may be a dream of someone who has died, which feels impossibly real, or a predictive dream, which shouldn't be possible at all.

This kind of dream experience could be enough to rouse

your curiosity and make you wonder about all the dreams you don't remember. Then, dreaming is all about making your life even better.

But if your life is completely out of balance, the need is urgent and the call can be brutal. When I first heard my call to dreams, I thought they were trying to kill me.

I could see the tops of the fir trees on the far side of the road moving like weeds in fast water. They were lit from below by a yellow street lamp, but that was as far down as I could allow myself to look.

When I was seven, my mother took me to see Swan Lake at Wimbledon Theatre. It was the first time she had ever suggested we do something on our own together. She often took Susan out on her own but then Susan was sensible, well-behaved, hard-working and also brave, never complaining about having to do her injection every day. She was everything I should be, but wasn't. This was a self-evident fact even if nobody said it, and I accepted it without question.

I had never been inside a theatre before, and we sat high up at the back, watching the tiny ballerinas flit like fairies across the stage. They were sparkles in a well of light, with invisible people peering in from the darkness above.

My mother was entranced by the ballet but I couldn't follow the story. I wasn't a frilly frocks kind of girl and I couldn't understand why she had chosen this moment, and this event, but I felt I was being given something mysterious and important.

The precipitation of this mystery was the musical jewellery box my mother gave me a few weeks later for my eighth birthday. It was covered in soft creamy leather with a gold patterned border pressed into it and a golden clasp. When you opened the lid, a little ballerina snapped upright on a red velvet stage and began to turn.

She went fast at first, and then gradually slowed down as the dying swan faltered towards its last hesitant notes and she wobbled into her final turn. The musical box had a key, and that made it a perfect hiding place. All I needed was a secret to hide in it.

I began collecting things I could use to kill myself with. I didn't seem to need a reason for doing this – it was just another collection like my button box and cigarette cards of wild animals. There was a rusty razor blade I found in the bathroom bin, two slightly eroded white tablets someone had left on the kitchen dresser and a twist of brown parcel string.

From time to time, I would take these objects out and look at them, turning them over and over in my hands. They were not attached to any function in the real world any more than the buttons in my button box were for sewing onto garments or the animals on the cigarette cards for catching on safari. They were simply objects, but being secret made them magical. They filled me with an exhilaration of wonder and fear.

It is said that the movement of air from a butterfly flapping its wings can eventually lead to a tornado on the other side of the world, but the circumstances have to create the right conditions. It works in the same way as sound, where the strength and effect of a musical note, reverberating through time and space, depends upon such things as wind and weather, and any other noises and distractions that get in the way. The ballerina's secret may never have led to the tornado if circumstances had been different.

When I started my collection we had just moved to a larger

house, and not long after that the vicar called. I wouldn't have noticed except that his visit caused a big argument.

'Who was that?' my mother asked, coming out of the kitchen, wiping her hands on a tea towel. My father had just shut the front door.

'The sky pilot from across the road.'

I could tell by the way he said it that my father did not like vicars.

'What did he say?' asked my mother.

'Welcome to the parish.'

'That's nice. Why didn't he come in?'

'I told him we're not interested. We're all atheists here.'

My mother was angry.

'How could you say that? Some of us aren't atheists. Some of us are agnostics. And anyway, you shouldn't be rude to a vicar.'

My father didn't see why he had to be polite. Religion was the greatest evil ever invented by man, it had caused the most wars and its whole purpose was to keep the common people down. My mother protested that she wasn't talking about religion but God, and just because the church was part of the powers-that-be that didn't mean God did not exist.

'Well show me the proof that God exists then,' said my father.

'If I could do that I'd be a believer and not an agnostic.'

My mother went back to the kitchen and my father pursued her, refusing to let it go. In his opinion being an agnostic was almost more indefensible than being a believer. At least believers had the courage to have convictions, even though their convictions were wrong.

Eventually, my mother backed down. My father said he was the voice of the modern world and she was stuck in the past.

It was the dawn of the 1960's and people were closing their doors on vicars all over the country. They were turning their backs on old superstitions and facing forward to a future lit by the clear light of science.

Listening at the door, I picked up several scraps of information which confused and unsettled me. One, there were people who believed there was no God. Two, there were people who thought there might be a God but they weren't sure. Three, these people were my parents. I had never given any thought to the question of whether there was a God. I had made assumptions.

For the first time in my life, I thought my parents must be wrong. But this seemed so unlikely that I didn't want to challenge them directly, deciding instead to talk to Susan. Susan was very clever – she had just passed her eleven-plus exam, which proved it.

'Daddy thinks there isn't any God, but that's not right is it?'

'Of course it's right,' she said. 'Only little kids believe in God. He's made up, like Father Christmas.'

If Susan said God didn't exist then it must be right, although a world without God made no more sense to me than a song without sound.

My immature belief in God became another secret, like the one in the ballerina's box, intense at first but fading as the grown-up world grew stronger. Over the following years, I gradually understood that you couldn't really kill yourself with a rusty blade or two aspirin tablets or a piece of parcel string, and God couldn't really exist if there was no scientific proof.

I understood it, but I couldn't feel it, and my father's angry dogmatism during my teenage years set up a strong resistance in me, which reactivated my belief. While my friends argued with their parents about what time they had to be home and whether their skirt was too short, all my rows with my father were about such things as what happened when you died and whether angels existed.

I didn't know anyone religious and I'd never set foot in a church, except once when someone at our youth club got confirmed, so when my father challenged me for proof, I didn't know how to argue it. By the time the famous American evangelist, Billy Graham, came to London in 1966, I was ripe for conversion.

I went to see him in Wembley Stadium, on a youth club outing. I had never been part of such an enormous crowd, a hundred thousand people all enraptured, hanging on the preacher's every word, and when he called us to come down to the front and be saved, I was like a swimmer swept along on a wave.

After we had gone back to our seats, the preacher said that Jesus would always be with each and every one of us from now on, walking alongside us every step of the way. At that exact moment, I felt a hand on my shoulder. I nearly fell over. But when I turned round, I saw an unprepossessing boy of maybe nineteen with spots and a horrible haircut.

This boy was to be my mentor. He gave me a bunch of pamphlets and promised to help me stay on the path. I was fourteen years old; I had a mini skirt to just below my knickers, knee-high patent leather boots, jet black eyeliner and pale Pan Stik lips – even in the euphoric moment of being saved I knew there was no way I could have anything to do with a boy like him.

The pamphlets proved to be as disappointing as the mentor. There was no science, no proof, just a lot of dodgy dogma and dire warnings about hell. If that was the best that the greatest Christian road show on earth could come up with, then it felt like proof positive that God did not exist.

So it happened that Billy Graham finally won the argument that my father had never completely managed to win – a fact that neither of them would probably have appreciated.

When I was fifteen, Susan won an academic scholarship to go to university, the first person in the history of our family ever to have done so. I often went to stay with her at weekends, sleeping on the floor of her student room in the college building, a magnificent Gothic pile whose walls felt infused with ancient learning. She never actually asked me to visit; I just did.

When the time came for me to decide what to do after school I did what I always did, and followed Susan. I got a place at the same college in the same university, starting the September after she finished. But as I was packing my trunk to go, Susan's results arrived. It was almost impossible to believe – she had failed.

Royal Holloway College, Founder's Building,
when I went up in 1970

Instead of slip-streaming my perfect sister's trail of glory I found myself floundering in a sea of pointlessness. The only reason I had started on this academic path was that I thought Susan knew where it was going. How could she – brilliant, hard-working, sensible Susan – have flunked it? And how could I, who was none of those things, hope to succeed?

But it was too late to turn back and anyway, I didn't have a Plan B, or rather, all my Plan B's had been blown out of the water. Since primary school, I had always dreamt of becoming an artist when I grew up, and when I was at secondary school I took Saturday classes at the local art school.

I imagined myself doing book illustrations, or designing butter-packets, or creating beautiful pottery, but when it came to the crunch everyone said I would be mad to choose art school over university.

Susan had wanted to be a musician, all the way through school. She had played in youth orchestras in Moscow and Vienna, but she had done the sensible thing; she had given up her dreams, and gone to university to get a degree so that she would have a good job with security and a pension at the end.

She had done the sensible thing, and I had copied her, and now I found myself living in a student room two doors along the corridor from the one she had inhabited. I went to lectures and read books and passed time in the Students' Union building, but I had absolutely no idea why I was doing it.

And so, one thing led to another – the flutter of the plastic ballerina's skirt, the death of God, the fall of Susan. The wind blew through the echoing void. It sucked me out of my room in the college building and brought me shivering onto the parapet, four floors up.

I could feel the cold concrete under my bare feet and the

window at my back. I could see the tops of the fir trees on the far side of the road moving like weeds in fast water. They were lit from below by a yellow street lamp, but that was as far down as I could allow myself to look.

If I were to look directly down at the road so far beneath I might not be able to stop myself from stepping off. There would be a rush of air, the sound of my body slamming into the tarmac and then there would be blackness.

When I imagined the blackness I realised that my eyes were closed; when I tried to open them, I could not. That was how I knew I was asleep and that this was just a dream. With a surge of relief I opened my eyes, but I did not wake to find myself in bed.

I woke to find that I really was shivering on the parapet, looking down at the slick black pavement in the wet November night. My skin felt cold under my flimsy nightdress, and empty as if there was nothing inside it. I tried to breathe, but the air stayed outside.

I must have opened the window in my sleep and climbed out. Shaking uncontrollably, I eased myself down to a sitting position, edged my legs back over the sill and dropped down onto my bed. The air came rushing in.

I had been having these dreams for weeks now – like the one where I put my finger in the light socket and flicked the switch, or the one where I turned on the heater in my student room and didn't light the gas – dark dreams of suicide, calling me down. I had thought they would go away if I ignored them, but I couldn't ignore them any more.

First thing in the morning, I went to see the college doctor.

'My dreams are trying to kill me,' I said.

Not surprisingly, the doctor sent me to see the psychiatrist, who happened to be holding a clinic in the college medical centre that day. She asked me, 'How long have you been feeling depressed?'

The psychiatrist was not at all what I had expected. I thought a psychiatrist should be a man, for one thing. A man with a bald head who would look at you over half-glasses whilst posing incisive questions and making wise pronouncements.

'I'm not depressed,' I said. 'I'm just having terrible dreams.'

There was a long silence. Over the next few years, I got used to psychiatrists' silences, but so early on, I felt unnerved.

'So...' the psychiatrist said at last. 'Why don't you tell me a little bit more about these dreams?'

A psychiatrist should wear a white coat with a top pocket full of pens, but this one, with her tweed skirt, sensible shoes and no-nonsense short grey hair, would not have looked out of place at a WI tea party. She had a kindly face and I almost felt tempted to tell her about the dreams, but I decided not to.

The Interpretation of Dreams by Sigmund Freud was on my reading list and although I hadn't read it, because it was basically unreadable, I had leafed through a primer on Freudian thought.

I therefore knew that a psychiatrist could find out your darkest secrets from your dreams – secrets you didn't even know yourself and wouldn't want to know, because otherwise why would you have had to suppress them? These secrets were possibly incestuous and certainly sexual. 'So you put your finger in the light socket... hmm...'

'I don't want to talk about my dreams,' I said. 'I just want them to stop.'

'These bad dreams will be a symptom of your depression, so if we treat the depression, they should go away.'

'But I'm not depressed.'

Long silence. Trill of robin outside the window, chatter of students in college scarves, crossing the bright chilly quad. The psychiatrist leafed through her notes.

'Your doctor says these dreams you've been having are about committing suicide,' she said. 'Are you telling me that you have not been experiencing suicidal thoughts during the day?'

Well, yes – I had considered killing myself, but not in any dramatic kind of way, not because I felt desperate or even particularly unhappy. It was a rational thing – if life was pointless, which on balance it seemed to be, why should a person bother to go on with it?

Long silence, anticipation of life-changing insight, in-coming disappointment.

'There is this new approach to treating depression they're trialling in Australia, but it's very early days...'

I was going to protest again that I wasn't feeling depressed, but then she said the magic word.

'It's called the sleeping cure.'

The cure involved taking enough sleeping pills to fell a rhinoceros and topping them up round the clock, so that the patient stayed under for several days. By the time they woke up, they would theoretically have forgotten all about what made them unhappy and emerge into a brand new world.

I liked the sound of this because, as well as involving serious sleep, it had to be done under supervision and that meant I would have to stay in one of the medical centre rooms. The medical centre was on the ground floor.

That evening, I settled into one of the three in-patient rooms and the sister gave me the first dose. I fell into a deep pit of dreamless sleep. From time to time I surfaced, became aware *of people moving about, sat up to eat toast and go to the bathroom and then was given the next lot of tablets.*

When I finally woke up properly, it was indeed like waking up in a different world, a slightly blurry world with all the edges knocked off.

The psychiatrist stabilised me on a cocktail of chemicals designed to knock me out at night and get me up in the morning. The dreams stopped and I was able to function again. I read books, wrote essays, hung around the students' union, went out with boys, although it felt as if someone else was doing all those things.

When I graduated, they offered me a place to do a PhD. I applied for funding with all the joy and enthusiasm I might have felt if I was applying for a place in prison, but I didn't have any other ideas.

It's sobering to reflect now that if I had kept taking the tablets, I would probably have been able to go on that way for years, perfectly adapted to a world without dreams.

> **Compliance carries with it a sense of futility for the individual, and is associated with the idea that nothing matters and that life is not worth living. In a tantalising way, many individuals have experienced just enough of creative living to recognise that for most of their time they are living uncreatively, as if caught up in the creativity of someone else, or of a machine.**
>
> **DW Winnicott**

Conforming to the values and demands of the ordinary world may feel safe and sociable, but it comes at a cost to the individual. The call to dreams is a yearning towards reconnection with lost, abandoned or undiscovered parts of the authentic self. But answering the call means opening the door to whatever is moving beneath the surface, and you won't always like what comes up.

In the first adult writing workshop I ever taught, we began by making a collage, simply choosing images, words and patterns that appealed to us. One person chose a full-page picture of a big old piece of furniture, which was like a floor-to-ceiling, oak bookcase with little square drawers instead of shelves. It took up most of her paper, and she didn't want to overlap the edges, so there was hardly any room for anything else. When she saw what the others had done, she said, 'I don't like mine. It isn't me. I don't know why I chose that picture, but I wish I hadn't.'

Everything that comes up when you open the door is you, even when you don't like it. In a more recent workshop, a very confident and experienced writer was reluctant to share her story because she had created a character who disgusted her. She did read it out, because a lot of what we do in workshops is about sharing our stories, and it was a very powerful piece of writing.

You may write stories that upset or frighten you, that disgust or delight. The point is, you don't know the shadowy contents of the unconscious mind until you let them out. That can be scary and you may come up against objections, blocks and excuses.

Sometimes, a course participant who is normally happy to do all the exercises will balk at one, saying something like, 'I always react badly to being told what to do,' when they patently don't. There's information in our resistance, and the places you don't want to go may be the most fruitful seams to mine.

If you are feeling the 'call to dreams' but are having problems getting started with writing or dream-recalling, look for the true feelings and attitudes that lie behind what appear to be practical difficulties. Find out what fears may be holding you back.

Here's a little exercise that might help.

'I don't want to because...'

Write stream-of-consciousness for three minutes starting, 'I don't want to recall my dreams because...' Keep your pen moving on the paper, just writing whatever thoughts come into your head.

After three minutes, take another three minutes to write whatever it is that you haven't said.

Now reread what you have written as if it started, 'I don't want to write because...' Quite often whatever blocks you from remembering dreams is the same as what stops you from writing.

Although you might lose your nerve and refuse the call in the early stages, once you have experienced the wonder and magic of your inner stories, you will want to keep coming back, and that desire is what will help you to overcome any resistance or fear.

Try this little exercise to feel the energy within that desire.

'I want to write stories about...'

Write stream-of-consciousness for three minutes starting, 'I want to write stories about...'. Keep your pen moving on the paper, writing down what kind of stories you would like to write, what situations and characters and settings. Don't ponder – just write the first things that come into your head, even if they feel preposterous.

After three minutes, take another three minutes to write whatever it is that you haven't said.

Reread with this in mind: if you remembered more of your dreams, you would find stories among them about situations, characters and settings similar to the ones you want to write.

No number of courses can engage with your inner world for you; they can only show you what needs to be done and bring you to the door. No one else can go there with you. The journey into your inner world, whether through dreaming or writing, is a journey you have to make alone.

When we limit life to the conscious perception, ignoring the power of the symbols of the inner self, we miss the depth, the flavour, the colour and texture of our full selves.

Mary Jo McCabe

Most people are wholly identified with the conscious perception of life. They don't experience their dreams. They have dreams every night, but are oblivious to them.

In this way of being in the world, there is only what we consciously perceive, and oblivion; there is no experience in between. Sleep and death are the same thing – impenetrable darkness.

In our culture, we're afraid of dying. We go round and round like the ballerina, always on the move, looking straight ahead, trying to ignore the fear and fascination with death which lies beneath.

We may toy with it, we may flirt with it by getting 'dead drunk' or 'out of it' on drugs, or in the exquisite moment of 'the little death' of orgasm. We may plunge headlong into it on a wave of prescription drugs. We are drawn to oblivion, but only as a cessation of consciousness, not as a gateway to a different realm of being.

James Hillman, in *Dreams and the Underworld*, describes dreaming in terms of sinking down, of dropping below the surface into the realm of death.

Choosing to engage with dreams is like a kind of suicide. We let go of the waking 'I' and the ordinary world, and willingly become the dream 'I', walking the underworld. In this way, the dream 'I' is like the soul – it lives on after ego awareness is gone. The call to dreams is a call to soul.

Writing fiction is similar to dreaming, but less intense. We enter the 'writer's trance' and become, to some extent, our characters. We live in their lives, and grapple with their circumstances. But we are still aware of our own physical body, sitting at our desk, dipping in and out of the writing dream to answer the phone, pick up emails or make coffee.

Through dreaming and writing we can experience the 'colour and texture of our full selves' but in order to do that, we have to let go of our small idea of who we are and what life is. We have to let go of our need for control, and be prepared to accept whatever characters and images we find in the inner world.

If you aren't ready you simply won't be able to tap the full power of your inner self in your writing or establish dream-recall – your doubts and resistance will keep you safe.

2 Entering the House of Dreams

> To go in this direction, we must sever the link with
> the dayworld, foregoing all ideas that originate there
> – translation, reclamation, compensation. We must go
> over the bridge and let it fall behind us, and if it will
> not fall, then let it burn.
>
> James Hillman

If we remember dreams, especially frightening or unsettling ones, our first instinct is to rationalise them away. 'It was only a dream,' we tell ourselves, when we wake up in a sweat or in tears. 'I know why I dreamt about my loved one dying,' we say. 'I know what that image represents.'

The instinct to rationalise is a sort of self-preservation. Instead of losing our self in the dream-world we colonise and plunder our dreams for evidence that supports or expands our ideas about who we are and how the world works.

Almost invariably, when we decide we want to engage more fully with our dreams it's with a view to interpreting them. Our most popular dream books are symbols dictionaries; our dream experts are not shamans but therapists, and what we seek from them is not a better understanding of dreams but a better understanding of waking life.

Dreams can indeed be a rich source of insights into

waking life, but starting with that focus is like trying to engage with creative writing through learning techniques. It puts the cart before the horse.

With writing, first find out what stories are inside you and want to come out. Write, write, write – keep writing and your style and technique will develop naturally, so that any technical information you may pick up along the way will be easy to understand, assess and assimilate.

People can write great books with absolutely no technical training at all, but no one ever wrote a great book without finding their passion and learning to tap the mysterious processes of their psyche.

With dreams, start with the dreaming. Immerse yourself. Find out what the dream-world is and how it works, then you will gradually and naturally develop a sense of how and where it relates to your waking life. Any theories and ideas about interpretation after that will be easier to weigh up in the context of what you have learnt from experience.

If you want to enter the House of Dreams, or 'go over the bridge', as James Hillman puts it, you have to leave behind theories and dictionaries; you have to lay aside even the intention of interpreting, at least until you start to know the territory.

The point about the dream-world is that it's much bigger than waking consciousness. As Einstein said, knowledge is limited, but imagination is not. Ideas that originate in the day-world are limited by our current understanding – for example, our cultural concept of ourselves is defined by psychological theories. In the dream-world, the possibilities are infinite.

Any attempt to try to understand dreams using our

rational, day-world mind will be reductive and distorting. At best, we're likely to come away feeling frustrated and discouraged; at worst, we may find meanings in our dreams that aren't really there.

Approaching dreams armed with a symbols dictionary and a set of psychological assumptions, which is the way most people try to do it, is like trying to use a Portuguese phrase book on a trip to Istanbul. Even worse, it's like doing so believing Portuguese to be the language of Istanbul, so you don't understand why you can't work out what anyone is saying.

And if you do that, you aren't really entering the dream at all, but keeping your feet firmly planted in the waking world.

I was sitting at the wheel of a car but I didn't know how to drive. I heard a sound from the back of the car. I looked in the rear-view mirror and there was a man. He had a knife in his hand...

The second psychiatrist I saw was a man. He was tweedy and mild-mannered like the one I had seen at university a few years before, but he seemed more like the real thing. Maybe it was the half-glasses that did it, or the tape recorder whirring on the desk between us, or the fact that I saw him in a proper consulting room. Maybe it was the bleakness of the situation that meant I needed to believe in him.

I thought about Susan all the time. I wondered when she first had the idea of killing herself. Had she had a secret like the ballerina's stash when she was little too? Had she had the dark dreams, and had they brought her out of her student bed onto the high parapet in the dead of the night?

And what did it feel like, that moment when she had decided to keep swallowing the tablets and not stop? Suddenly the friendly bottles on the shelf didn't seem like the key to coping with life – they had been her key to the door of death. I did not want to follow her through it.

As soon as I stopped taking all the tablets I was on, my life fell apart. My body felt unstable, rocked by tremors that seemed to constantly threaten a major quake. I abandoned my PhD plans and went north with my college sweetheart, who was now my husband.

A year after Susan's death, we were living in the Shetland Isles, way off the north coast of Scotland. He was teaching, and I was still struggling to hold myself together. I had panic attacks in the day and sleepless nights, but I absolutely refused to take any medication.

Worse than anything else, the dreams were back, terrifying nightmares which ripped me out of sleep, sweating and shaking. They didn't come every night, but often enough for me to be afraid of going to sleep.

This time around, the nightmares weren't about killing myself – they were about a killer coming after me with a knife. I dreamt he was prowling outside my door; he was chasing me across the open ground behind our house; he was stalking me, hiding in shadows.

The knifeman pursued me into my waking life as well, so that I would think I could hear his footsteps behind me or catch glimpses of him out of the corner of my eye. I felt frightened all the time. The knifeman was the reason why I found myself in a psychiatrist's office again.

This psychiatrist wore a comfy brown cardigan with leather buttons and a pair of scuffed lace-up shoes, and his battered briefcase was full of dog-eared notes. His presence in the consulting room made it feel somehow hushed and dusty like an old library.

In that space it felt all right not to fill the silences and I sat looking down at my knees, or staring out of the window at the slate-grey sea. I was so full of emotions that I couldn't seem to feel anything at all, and so full of questions that I didn't know what to ask. The psychiatrist didn't push me. From time to time he took a pack of indigestion tablets out of his briefcase and put one in his mouth.

'What are you thinking now, Jennifer? Is there something you would like to say?'

I wanted to talk about Susan, the ballerina, the parapet; I wanted to tell him about the secret stash of sleeping tablets I still had hidden in my drawer, just in case. I wanted to ask him how it was possible to trust the people you loved most in the world not to suddenly kill themselves and abandon you for ever.

'What about your parents?'

'I don't know. They're just my parents.'

I wanted to talk about the mind-numbing tedium of school and university, to ask him how it was possible to trust life to support you and not let you fall into a dark pit of pointlessness. Sometimes I tried, but he seemed to think I was avoiding the real issue.

'Let's talk about your mother.'

Up here in the islands the silences were filled with the rush of the wind sweeping along the side of the building or the rattle of rain billowing in from the sea; the disembodied wailing of gulls over the water.

'How do you feel about your father?'

I had lots of feelings about my mother and father but I didn't want to talk about them because they didn't feel urgent or relevant. Your parents were your parents; they were just there, like the sea, *like the sky. The psychiatrist popped another indigestion tablet.*

'*Tell me about these dreams.*'

I wanted to talk about the knifeman but I knew what he would say. 'Aha… I see… the man has a knife and he's standing outside your door…'

After half a dozen sessions of questions and silences the psychiatrist suggested that I write down every dream I could remember during the coming week. I wasn't keen. I never had any dreams except the ones about the knifeman and I certainly did not want to write those down.

But what did I have to lose? I put a notepad and pen beside my bed and waited for the dreams to come.

One of my early dream diaries –
made for me by my young husband

As soon as I started focusing on my dreams I found they came cascading through, four or five every night, loud and clear like a radio signal when you tune the dial. To my surprise, most of them were not nightmares, but strange and beguiling stories.

In my eyes the psychiatrist morphed from mousy librarian to amazing magician. Look in the hat, he had said, see what happens – and suddenly every kind of coloured silk had started streaming out.

For the next few sessions, I read all my dreams to the psychiatrist and he listened, nodded, considered. He only stopped me if there was something in a particular dream he wanted to talk about. I felt like a constable reading my notes to a great detective who was specially trained to sift through reams of routine enquiries and identify the important detail.

'I was in my room – the bedroom I shared with Susan. My bed was under a sort of awning, but the rest of the room was uncovered. It was raining hard. Susan's bed and most of our things were soaked.

'I went across to the window in the rain, and looked out at the garden. It was bathed in sunlight. There were beautiful coloured buildings at the end of it that I had never seen before, and beyond the far wall, a huge pink castle. I couldn't tell if it was real or a painted backdrop...'

The psychiatrist nodded me on.

'I was on a beach with high rocky cliffs behind. I began to climb up them but then I reached a point where I couldn't go on. I was trapped on a narrow ledge. Far below I could see people looking up. Above me were the towers of the University of Life. I went on and began a course there but I was disappointed because it was only exercises in translating Chinese into French and I was bored...'

He considered; he nodded.

'My mother was going to make a tunic for me out of a piece of bright orange towelling with strawberries sewn on. How was she going to be able to sew them on? It puzzled me...'

He made a note; he nodded me on.

'I was sitting at the wheel of a car but I didn't know how to drive. I heard a sound from the back of the car. I looked in the rear-view mirror and there was a man. He had a knife in his hand. I tried to open the door but it was stuck...'

'Was this man somebody you knew?'

'I couldn't see his face properly. I was too scared to look.'

'What do you think the knife might represent?'

I gradually understood that the important dreams were the violent or sexual ones so although I went on recording everything, I only read out the ones I thought the psychiatrist would want to hear. Maybe the reason he had so far not explained what any of my dreams might mean was because there had simply been too many. If I only read one or two, he would have more time to tell me what they meant.

But he didn't tell me; he just asked more and more questions.

'Why do you think you dreamt about Idi Amin?'

'I don't know.'

'What qualities do you associate with Idi Amin?'

'I don't know. He's just a dictator and he threw the Asians out of Uganda.'

'Hmm... a dictator... a powerful man...'

Long silence. He seemed to be waiting for me to come to his conclusions on my own, but I only had a rough idea of what his conclusions were, and I just felt more and more frustrated.

'You know what these dreams mean and I don't, so why can't you just tell me?'

But the psychiatrist was inscrutable. 'It's not my dream' was all he would say.

I found him frustrating but I trusted him. I believed he knew what he was doing. He had certainly known that simply deciding to remember my dreams and write them down would unleash this torrent of dream material, even though he was still refusing to let me have the code.

Since the psychiatrist was taking so long to start telling me what my dreams meant I decided to try and work it out for myself in the meantime. As soon as I bought my dictionary of dream symbols I wondered why I hadn't thought of this before. It all looked quite straightforward.

The psychiatrist had noted that the knifeman was always outside, never actually sticking the knife in, and this seemed to suggest to him some kind of forbidden sexual urge. The fact that the knife must be phallic was absolutely taken as read.

According to the dictionary, a knife did mean an erect penis because it penetrated the flesh – but then, according to the dictionary, so did a sewing needle because the act of sewing was like coitus, the needle piercing the fabric in an up-and-down, in-and-out movement.

The knife-as-penis explanation felt wrong for the knifeman because there was absolutely no sexual feeling in the knifeman dreams, just screams and terror and danger lurking outside. The needle-as-penis didn't throw much light on the dream riddle of how my mother was going to be able to sew the strawberries onto the orange tunic in my earlier dream either.

I flicked back through my dream diaries looking for that dream. I had half a dozen exercise books full of tightly packed writing now – it wasn't my usual style but I somehow felt the need to write tiny when it came to dreams, and to use pencil rather than biro so that the words could be quite faint.

Orange, according to the symbols dictionary, was the colour of Buddhist robes and signified occult power; a jacket or tunic, in a woman's dream, meant the loving protection of a man. Strawberries weren't in the dictionary, but fruit signified a more mature phase of life. A long fruit such as a banana was a penis – no surprises there – and round fruits such as apples stood for breasts. Soft fruits such as peaches were female genitalia, so it seemed likely that strawberries would be too.

When I applied the logic of the symbols dictionary to my dreams it made my brain hurt, but I pushed on, convinced that sooner or later I would find one that clicked and then I would understand how to do it. I thought it would be like the process of understanding how simultaneous equations worked or Latin grammar – months of feeling about in the dark eventually broken by a slow or sudden dawn of understanding.

But the more I persevered, the more confused I became, especially when the symbols book talked about archetypes. Lots of everyday things could be archetypes as well as having their ordinary interpretations, so I was always coming up against the problem of trying to understand what the book said about them.

In one of my dreams I was walking through a formal garden on a moonlit night when a snowy owl flew down. I saw it catch a mouse. According to the symbols dictionary the garden was the dreamer's personality and the moon was intuition; the mouse was a diffident person and the owl was wisdom.

If that didn't add up to a confusing enough explanation, a garden could also represent the mother archetype, the moon in a woman's dream could be the Animus and the owl in a man's dream the Anima – for all of which the book said I should see the section on archetypes.

The pages about archetypes were the first ones to come loose and fall out, I flicked through them so often and so fretfully. There was the Ego, the Shadow, the Anima, the Animus, the Self: in a woman's Self, the great mother, the mother, the terrible mother, the princess, the seductress, the amazon, the huntress, the priestess and the sorceress; in a man's Self, the wise old man, the father, the ogre, the youth, the tramp, the hunter, the hero, the villain and the trickster.

The headings were easy enough to grasp but the explanations were not, and trying to understand what they meant in the context of a dream was completely beyond me.

I didn't tell the psychiatrist I was trying to work out what my dreams meant on my own. There didn't seem much point as I wasn't getting anywhere with it and I thought he would be more likely to capitulate and come up with some interpretations if he believed he was the only chance I had.

I still only read the dreams I thought he would be interested in, and there were plenty of them now. The psychiatrist had started the resonance with his focus on violence and sex, and the more open I was the more strongly those themes came thundering through.

'In a war,' I read, 'six girl soldiers were standing in a pool. The enemy was advancing. What should they do? They could run, swim or hide beneath the surface. They ducked down, hiding, but they couldn't breathe, so they had to stand up. There were men with guns and the girl soldiers said, "Please don't shoot us; at least give us a chance."

'Then I stood up and said, "Since many on both sides are dead we should call a halt and discuss our differences." The enemy was in the house – not a man, not a woman, but a talking machine. It sat on a high throne. It threw a list of grievances.'

'Six...' the psychiatrist mused. I knew from my exhaustive reading of the symbols dictionary that six was sex, not just because it sounded similar but also it was the multiplication of the male and female numbers, three and two, though how they got to be the male and female numbers I hadn't the faintest idea. I didn't say anything.

'Soldiers – what comes to mind when you think of soldiers?'

What came to mind now was the dictionary meaning, 'obsessions'. I shrugged and said nothing. We moved on to the men with guns, of course, but skimmed over the talking machine.

We skimmed over more and more as time went on. The psychiatrist seemed to be less interested in my dreams now that I had got talking. I suspected that maybe the reason why he wasn't so keen any more and had always steadfastly held out against telling me what they meant might be because he actually didn't know. Maybe his magic only extended to pulling coloured silks out of hats, and once they were out he didn't know what to do with them.

After two years of the psychiatrist not telling me what my dreams meant, I was still feeling as confused as ever. Also, focusing hard on all the negative things in my past had mysteriously failed to make me feel any happier. I still didn't understand what had happened to Susan – we had barely talked about her – and I hadn't thrown away my secret stash.

But the panic attacks had stopped, I could sleep without pills and the knifeman had retreated back into my dreams. Although I still had nightmares about him he didn't seem to dominate my nights in the same way, because I knew he was only a small part of my whole dream life, and even when the nightmares came I found that tethering them to the page seemed to take away some of their power.

At our last session the psychiatrist asked if I was planning to go on recording my dreams. I told him I was.

'In that case, you might be interested in a book that's just come out,' he said, jotting down the details on a piece of paper. 'It won't help you to understand your dreams but it might give you some strategies for coping with the nightmares.'

That book was Creative Dreaming, *by Patricia Garfield.*

To go in the dark with a light is to know the light.
To know the dark, go dark. Go without sight,
And find that the dark, too, blooms and sings,
And is travelled by dark feet and dark wings.

Wendell Berry

A man saw his neighbour searching underneath the street light outside his house.

'Have you lost something?'

'I've dropped my keys.'

The man wanted to help.

'Where exactly did you drop them?'

His neighbour pointed into the shadows further down the lane.

'Over there,' she said. 'But it was too dark to find them so I'm looking over here.'

Trying to understand dreams in a rational way is looking in the wrong place. The key is in the darkness, beyond the light of reason. You have to step away from everything you think you know – your waking 'I' – and surrender yourself to the world of dreams.

This dream-world is a personal cornucopia of stories and adventures, inspirations and possibilities, available to everyone 24:7 from the cradle to the grave. Regular dream recall means you develop free and open access to the story-layer of yourself, and it's very easy to establish. All that it requires is faith, intention and practice.

You need to have faith that you will have some dreams and be able to recall them – although actually if you look into the evidence, you don't really need faith at all because dream studies consistently find that everyone has several periods of dreaming every night and that when people decide to recall their dreams, they do.

Deciding you will do it, making a clear intention, is what sets the thing in motion. I would suggest you intend to recall your dreams for a six-week period in the first instance. This isn't too great a commitment, but it gives you time to establish recall and start to familiarise yourself with your personal dream-world.

Some people find that regular dream-recalling, if they aren't used to it, can mean they feel less rested in the morning, but this settles down as you start to move more easily between dream and waking states, so it would be a shame to give up in the first few weeks.

Establishing dream-recall requires practice in the sense of developing a daily habit – time set aside and dedicated every morning. It often happens very quickly in these conditions but, if it doesn't start immediately, don't assume that nothing is happening. See it as a seed which is growing its roots first, invisible in the ground, and think, 'Any minute now, it will come through.'

If you aren't a regular dream-recaller and would like to give it a try, here are my suggestions to start you off. You can develop the details in ways that work best for you.

Recalling and recording dreams

Make your intention part of your waking life by reminding yourself from time to time during the day that you are going to remember your dreams and write them down.

When you go to bed:

- set your alarm at least fifteen minutes before your normal wake-up time
- if you're worried you might go back to sleep, set a second alarm for five minutes before your normal time
- put your notepad and pen beside your bed – this physical action is like a ritual that sets your intention to record. If you prefer, you can record into your phone or iPod and write your dream down later
- tell yourself, before you go to sleep, 'I will dream tonight, and I will recall my dream'
- tell yourself, 'I will record any dream or dream fragment I have, however random or uninteresting it may seem'
- go over the events of the day in your mind – your dream life and waking life are connected through your psyche in the moment
- run through last night's dream in your mind – this puts you in dream-mode, and can encourage follow-on dreams.

When you wake up in the morning:

- wake slowly into a quiet room with no TV or radio
- don't look at your texts/updates/messages until after you've recorded
- don't let your mind race forward to the concerns of the day
- don't open your eyes or turn on the light until you are ready to start recording
- lie in the position you woke up in until you have got all the dreams you can, then turn quietly into other favourite sleeping positions. One theory is that your body 'remembers', so adopting the position you were in when you had a particular dream can trigger recall
- even if you don't remember a dream, enjoy the daydreaming fantasies of your half-awake state. Sometimes they will take you straight back into your dreams, but anyway there is no qualitative difference between daydreams, night dreams and fantasies
- some complete dreams can present as single words or images rather than narratives so don't feel disappointed – draw or describe them as fully as possible
- notice when you start to interpret, and stop yourself – stay in the experience of the dream, not your ideas about it
- record something every morning.

This last point is the most important thing. If you don't have any dreams or waking fantasies to record, write stream-of-consciousness for ten minutes, keeping the pen moving on the paper continuously, recording any random thoughts that come into your head.

Even if all you manage is ten minutes along the lines of 'I can't remember any dreams, this is a waste of time, why am I doing it...?' you will have held the space. That will mean there's no incentive to forget your dreams another day because forgetting doesn't mean you can get out of doing the writing!

Dorothea Brande recommends a short period of daily writing in this free, unfocused way. She suggests setting your alarm half an hour early and writing anything that comes to you – dreams, fantasies, reflections; bits of conversation, real or imagined; examinations of conscience. Sixty years later, Julia Cameron made the same recommendation in *The Artist's Way*, calling the practice 'daily pages'.

Daily pages don't have to be written immediately upon waking but that's the best time, while your mind is still relaxed and open, poised between the dream and the demands of the waking world.

A stranger on a train that I was talking to about dreams told me she felt that trying to remember your dreams was like trying to catch eels in a barrel of oil – even if you caught one, it would usually slip between your fingers and disappear. Dream recalling and daily pages are the same practice: the writing will help you to catch those oily eels, and the eels will help to make your writing more exciting.

If you need a bit of support with recalling and recording, it can help to share dreams on a weekly basis with a group of friends. It doesn't matter if you don't have dozens of dreams to report – you only need to come up with a maximum of one or two dreams a week and if you haven't got that, you can share fragments, images, or even just your sense of what you might have been dreaming.

Sharing dreams is immensely enjoyable and setting up a group can be a great idea, even if you have no difficulty with daily recall, but someone has to hold the focus of the group or you can easily slip into interpretation. Creative dream-sharing is about telling the stories of your adventures in the dream-world – it has nothing to do with understanding waking life.

So, in a group situation, treat dreams as a completely different area of experience, not seeking to analyse things that happen in the dream-world any more than you would analyse the stories of waking life. For example, if I told you I had just had scrambled eggs for breakfast, you would not be asking yourself, 'Why eggs? What's the significance of them being scrambled?' It just happened.

Tell your dreams like anecdotes; hear other people's dreams in the same way.

Creative dream-sharing

I think the ideal group size is between four and eight people.

The first thing you need to do in order to make the group feel safe is to agree what level of confidentiality you want. Is it OK to talk outside the group about a dream someone else has brought so long as you don't name names? Or does everyone prefer not to talk about other people's dreams outside the group at all? Begin every session with a reminder about what you have agreed.

The second thing is to make sure you all look after your own personal safety. Agree not to share in the group anything which makes you feel vulnerable or embarrassed. Treat dream experience in the same way as waking experience when it comes to choosing what you want to share.

Avoid sharing anything which seems to have an obvious link with your waking life concerns and problems. Be focused on the fact that this is not a therapy group, and choose instead whatever feels like the most interesting or exciting dream experience of the week.

Start with each person briefly summarising their dreams over the week and then share one or two dreams each. As the group develops, you will be able to devise dreaming tasks and adventures to experiment with together.

When you share a dream you are telling someone about something interesting that happened to you, and the rules are the same as when you tell stories from waking life.

Telling your dream:

- keep it brief – people can ask if they want more information
- make it interesting – just enough description and detail
- don't share anything that makes you feel embarrassed or uncomfortable.

Listening to someone else's dream:

- don't try to relate the dream to the dreamer's waking life any more than you would try to relate the story to a writer's life in a writing group

- you will get a sense of the dreamer in the dream in the same way as you get a sense of the writer in a piece of creative writing, but what is interesting is the story
- notice if you start to stray into interpretations and steer away
- be clear in your mind that any interpretations you make are reflections of your own beliefs and experiences, not the dreamer's.

Sharing dreams, whether in a group or briefly over the breakfast table, isn't just a pleasure and a privilege; it's a way of honouring and paying attention to your inner life, and anything you pay attention to will grow.

> **The experienced soul is connected to the observation of specifics. It has nothing to do with generalisations, standard types, intellectual classifications and habitual judgements.**
>
> **Shaun McNiff**

You cannot enter the House of Dreams armed with preconceived ideas, cultural assumptions and stock interpretations. When you step over the threshold, you are in a completely different world, which works by different rules, and speaks a different language.

You have to enter with your eyes and ears wide open, and focus on 'the observation of specifics'. The task is to notice everything and judge nothing. To take in all the details without trying to tie them into a narrative that makes sense to your waking mind.

One of the reasons we don't do this is because it can feel frightening. In the dream-world, bad and extreme things can happen, things we would never be exposed to in waking life; rationalising and categorising dreams are ways of cutting them down to size and taking away their power.

If you want to experience the full power and reality of the dream-world you have to leave these normal protections behind, but you don't have to go unprotected. You can learn appropriate dream skills for handling danger and fear.

3 The Beast in the Basement

The most important thing to remember during your
dream is fearlessness of dream images.

Patricia Garfield

I f you don't regularly recall your dreams you might think
your dream-world consists mostly of nightmares, because
scary or distressing dreams are the ones you're most likely
to remember. You might feel alarmed by the idea of
deliberately setting out to remember your dreams without
a therapist on hand to interpret them and make them feel
safe.

In my view, it can be less challenging to explore your
dreams in an open non-interpretative way, on your own or
with a group of fellow dream-travellers. Linking dreams to
your day-world, as we do in therapeutic situations, can
actually make their contents feel more unsettling and
disturbing. 'Why am I having this dream – what's wrong
with me – what should I do about it...?'

If you wake from a dream thinking, 'Aha – I know what
that was about!' then you're probably right, but when you
first start recalling and recording dreams most of them don't
seem to have any obvious connection with the day-world
and some, such as predictive dreams, may actually not be
connected with what's happening in your present life at all.

There's a danger that if you have to work at it to find the connections you might find meanings in your dreams which aren't really there, and that could distort your choices and decisions in waking-life. Finding the connections is an instinct that develops through experience; if you're striving, that's probably coming from an intellectual need to know.

I have had several therapists in my dream groups who have had experience of working with clients' dreams, and they have expressed surprise and pleasure at how liberating it can be to let go of looking for explanations in the day-world, to listen to other people's dreams and tell their own as pure experience for the self.

Other group participants have remarked that it feels much less exposing to share dreams when they're not worrying, 'What does this say about me?', and that positive effect spreads over into how they feel about sharing their writing.

However, you do need some sort of protection if you are going to be able to lay aside your interpretative armour. There could be monsters lurking in your House of Dreams and you may be driven back by fear unless you arm yourself with tools and techniques for tackling the beast in the basement.

'This is my dream,' I kept saying to myself. 'This is my dream, this is my dream!'

I read Creative Dreaming *in a single sitting. I couldn't put it down. It had never occurred to me before that there might be other ways to look at dreams except as coded messages from the unconscious mind.*

I had assumed that the whole point of remembering and recording dreams was to get information about things a person might have repressed or forgotten, which might explain whatever issues they were having in their waking life.

The problem with the psychological approach, as I had found, was that dreams never seemed to fit the interpretations you came up with, and even a psychiatrist couldn't necessarily come up with anything better. It might be fine in theory, but in practice it felt frustrating and made my brain hurt.

Patricia Garfield's book had absolutely nothing to do with the psychological approach. It was about dream traditions from different times and places which didn't view dreams as providing insights into waking life but as a source of experience for the self.

Rather than trying to understand dreams, the book was about developing skills which would help people enjoy a better dream experience, which in turn would make them feel happier and more confident in waking life. The goal of dreaming was simply to make life better and one of the dream skills a person could acquire, which would certainly make my life better, was how to eradicate nightmares.

What if I didn't have to find out what the knifeman represented? What if I could fight him on his own turf, within the dream? That's what the section on the Malaysian Senoi tribe's dreaming tradition said you could do.

The Senoi method was very straightforward. You had to intend before you went to sleep that if you met any dream adversaries you would face them, look them in the eye, overcome them and find a reward. If you woke up before you had achieved a positive outcome you had to re-enter the dream, either asleep or awake, and finish the job.

It seemed implausible to me that a person could decide what to dream, and as for looking the knifeman in the eye, well that felt plain impossible. But the idea was in my head and straight away it started to affect my dreams. It also affected the way I recorded them.

Since I had started working with the symbols dictionary I had been writing my dreams in small blocks in the middle of the page like scientific specimens, subsequently surrounding them with red notes and arrows. Now they spread out again across the full width, not leaving any room for interpretations.

At first, it was as if my dreams were providing me with practice runs before the main event because the adversaries I met were not very frightening and getting rid of them was easy, as in the dream I called 'The smartly dressed intruder'.

In this dream, I dreamt 'I was going to visit two ancient sisters who lived in a tumbledown croft on one of Shetland's outer islands but when I arrived, I found they weren't there and the house had become derelict.

'The ceiling in the main room had fallen in and there were tea trays stuck over the gaps with slogans on them such as "I begin to despair". Each slogan was dated, so they were like a diary. Perhaps the sisters were dead? Or perhaps they had been taken away?

'I stayed in the croft because it was too late to go home. In the middle of the night, I heard an intruder. It was a small, smart, middle-aged woman. She was rifling through the cupboards, seemingly unaware that there was anyone else in the room. I sat up in bed and declared loudly that I was the headmistress of a large comprehensive school. The intruder was so shocked, she ran away.'

After I had faced up to several not very frightening dream

adversaries, I found myself encountering more scary ones. Most of them were wild animals like the dog-cat, which showed up in several dreams.

The first time I met the dog-cat I was walking in a garden where I knew I shouldn't be. A small dog or cat, an ugly little hybrid, started yapping around my ankles. I was frightened because its behaviour was so aggressive, I thought it might have rabies.

A second dog-cat came, much bigger than the first one, and I panicked. I began to run. Then suddenly, I turned to face them. I was wearing big boots and I made it very clear that I would kick them if they came any closer.

Confronting my dream adversaries did make me feel less fearful, and it had the added bonus of being enjoyable. As I got better at it, I realised I hadn't been remembering to do the second part – finding a reward. Simply becoming aware of the fact meant I started to do it in my dreams.

In 'Tackling the tiger' I dreamt 'I was hiding in the bathroom of my childhood home with Susan. The door was ajar and a tiger was guarding it to stop us getting away. I forced the tiger out into the hall, although I knew it might bite my hands off – I was prepared to suffer in order for Susan to get out.

'I pushed the tiger down onto the floor, grabbed a pillow and tried to stifle it. When it was subdued but still breathing, I saw some jewels and old photos on a shelf. I grabbed them and we ran away.'

After conquering middle-aged ladies and dog-cats, tigers and a host of other dream adversaries I started to feel it might actually be possible for me to confront the knifeman. Once this alarming idea was inside my head, it was only a matter of time before the knifeman came.

On the peat track across the bare hillside behind our house

I dreamt 'I was walking home across the bare peat hillside behind our house when I found a red high-heeled shoe. I recognised it because, in my dream, I had seen the other one on television the night before, on a news bulletin about a murder victim. There was a psychopathic killer on the loose and people had been warned not to go out alone. I knew I was in mortal danger.

'A man came running towards me at an oblique angle, as if he hadn't seen me. If I stayed still he might not notice me – but then if he did notice me it would be too late to run away. I realised he had a knife. I started running. He saw me and came after me. There was absolutely nowhere to hide.

'I stopped running and turned round. I ran towards the killer. He was so startled, he stopped. As we came face to face, I saw that he wasn't young. He was about my height and he had a deeply lined forehead. I couldn't look into his eyes. He had one hand around the knife and the other ready to grab my arm if I

tried to hit him with the shoe, which I was still holding in my hand. It was my only weapon.

'I couldn't attack him and I couldn't run away. All I could do was wait for him to make his move and try to defend myself if he went for me. I had to look him in the eye – it was the only way, but I just couldn't. All I saw was the lined forehead.' Sweating and trembling, I woke up.

The next day, I kept thinking about my encounter with the knifeman, how I had dared to turn and confront him, how I had nearly looked him in the eye and how I had failed. I forced myself to actually ask for another dream about the knifeman. I made a clear intention; when he came I would confront him, I would look him in the eye and I would win.

That night, I dreamt 'I was asleep in bed and the knifeman was in the house. I could feel his presence on the other side of the bedroom door. I lay stock still under the covers. I could scarcely breathe. If I was completely quiet, maybe he wouldn't know I was there. Maybe he would give up and go away.

'Then I thought, "He never goes away. I have to confront him, and make him go." So I got up out of bed. I went to the door. I turned the handle.

'He was standing in the hallway, with the knife in his hand. I felt a surge of panic rising. How could I have been so stupid? I wasn't even armed – what chance did I have against the knifeman?

'I needed a weapon. I looked on the hall table and there was a gun. "Of course," I thought, "this is my dream and I can put whatever I want in it!" I picked up the gun and pointed it at the knifeman's chest. As he started backing away, I lifted my eyes and looked into his face.

'"This is my dream," I kept saying to myself. "This is my dream, this is my dream!"

'I forced the knifeman out of the house and he sloped away into the shadows. I closed the front door. It was heavy and strong. I leant my back against it. "Now I should go on and find a reward," I thought. But I was so overwhelmed by what I had done that I could not do any more.'

Dreams call from the imagination to the imagination and can only be answered by the imagination.

James Hillman

Dreams are not processes of the conscious mind, and the rational skills of interpretation and explanation are therefore not effective ways to engage with them. The Senoi method works because it uses the appropriate power to overcome dream fears, and that is the power of the imagination.

The Senoi method makes you active rather than passive, in a position to choose what happens in your dreams. Once you have mastered it, you can enter the dream on its own terms, without fear, in full confidence that you'll be able to handle whatever you might find there

The beauty of this method is that it's easy. It works by pure intention, instructions from the waking self to the dream 'I', and does not require full lucidity within the dream. Once you have intended the pattern, your dream will follow it.

Like any dream-work, it requires practice, and it's important always to follow through with any upsetting or unsettling dream and bring it to a satisfying resolution, either by intending and going back to sleep, or in waking fantasy. In this way, you create the positive path you want all your dreams to follow.

Soon, this style of creative dreaming becomes automatic, so that you always tackle difficulties and achieve positive outcomes in your dreams, without having to specifically intend it every night before you go to sleep.

When I did a session on this technique with a group of other authors, one of them expressed reservations that it might reduce the range of emotions in her dreams; she valued frightening dreams as a resource for writing.

But the point and effect is not to eradicate difficult dream situations – it is to bring them to a resolution, in exactly the same way as we resolve the stories of fiction. You won't have fewer nightmares, and they won't be less scary, but you will push through the fear towards a creative resolution.

Knowing that you can do this actually enables you to go more fully into the dark places and feel the emotions, rather than waking up in the middle or neutralising the feelings with interpretations, or blocking your dreams out because you're afraid of having nightmares.

Creative dreaming doesn't only improve the quality of your dream-life – its positive effects spill over into your waking life, too. If dreams are seen as experience for the self, they offer opportunities for learning new skills and gaining fresh insights in the same way that waking life does, and the challenges they offer will be precisely relevant to the dreamer in the moment.

Dreams may even represent better opportunities for self-development than waking life because they give a much wider range of experience and the dreamer has far more freedom to choose how to engage with it. Dealing with difficult dream situations is a wonderful opportunity to experience yourself as a capable and successful person.

Creative dreaming – overcoming fear

I'd better say at the outset that this is not about trying to incubate a nightmare, but rather putting an intention in place about how to tackle it, should one occur. Several people in a recent dream group reported they had failed in their task because they had only had nice dreams that week, so I should evidently have been a bit clearer.

Before you go to sleep, make a firm intention that you will:

- confront and conquer dream adversaries– these may be anything from the monsters and psychopaths of nightmare to situations which provoke negative emotions such as disappointment, frustration or confusion

- if you can't overcome your dream adversary on your own, call on allies, special powers, weaponry – whatever it takes

- achieve a positive outcome – if you should wake up before a difficult dream experience is resolved, either intend to bring it to a positive outcome and go back to sleep, or complete it in waking fantasy. Re-enter the dream in your imagination, experiencing it as fully as you can, using your senses to feel your way back into it, and then imagine on towards a satisfying conclusion. Record this imagining-on afterwards, as part of your dream.

The Senoi have a dream-sharing session every morning, relating what they did in their dreams and discussing what they might have done in order to achieve the best outcome, in exactly the same way that people might discuss the events of waking life.

If you have a dream group, sharing dream experiences in this way can help you to notice when you are automatically tackling adversaries and achieving positive outcomes in your dreams, as this quickly becomes so natural that it happens on its own even when you haven't deliberately intended it.

When you are listening to a person's dream, watch out for the creative dream-resolving pattern. It might not be obvious, like in a full-blown nightmare. Facing up to frightening situations in your dreams filters down through to every level of fear, from heart-stopping terror to mild anxiety.

It might be overcoming stress, such as in a dream I had about having a meeting with my agent at a station when my train was about to come. I was panicking in case we didn't have time to get through the agenda but then I thought, 'This is my dream, so I'll just make the train come twenty minutes later!'

Or it might be calming a panic, such as one workshop participant's dream that she was floating down a swollen river on stone blocks. She suddenly realised that stone blocks didn't float, and started to panic. 'But it was OK because I said, "I am dreaming..."'

Watch for the pattern even when there isn't any 'this is my dream' moment of awareness. Another participant dreamt she was at a wedding, where a lovely girl was marrying a sinister man. She was dismayed for the girl, and wanted to stop her going through with it. Then one of the groom's friends got aggressive towards one of the bridesmaids, the bride's party turned on them, and the wedding was called off.

Another person in the same session dreamt her son had had a tattoo. This worried her, but she reassured herself in the dream, with the idea that he could have it removed by laser treatment, or that maybe it was just a transfer and not a proper tattoo at all.

You can experience what the Senoi approach feels like through creative writing.

Creative dream-writing

If you can remember a nightmare you've had in the past, write it out to the wake-up point, and then continue, bringing the story to a satisfying conclusion by facing and subduing your adversary and reaping your reward.

If you can't remember a bad dream or nightmare, you can create a new one through visualisation.

a) Start by making a list of all the common nightmare situations you can think of, such as drowning, being chased, being naked or inappropriately dressed, not being prepared for an exam...

Choose one from your list.

b) Close your eyes and take a few slow breaths, to ease

yourself into your inner space. Imagine yourself in this nightmare situation, just before the crisis. Are you alone? What are you doing there?

Are you indoors or outside? What time of day is it? What's the weather like? Use all your senses to fully experience the situation – what can you see, hear, touch, smell, taste?

Feel the fear – notice where it is in your body.

Now write the scene, to the point where you wake up in a cold sweat. Don't take more than about five minutes.

c) Put your pen down. Take a few slow breaths, and imagine yourself back in the dream. Again, use all your senses to really be there. Face up to the situation, and prepare to take action.

Overcome the enemy, difficulty or danger using allies, weapons or special powers if you need to. Remember that it doesn't have to be realistic or plausible – the rules of imagination apply.

Feel the emotions of struggle and triumph in your body, and look around for some kind of treasure or reward to bring back with you.

Take about ten minutes to write down the rest of the story.

If you do this with a group, you can feel the tension rising in the room as they begin to focus on nightmare situations. There will be a palpable atmosphere of anxiety as they write the first section, and then a release of energy and relief as they take control of the situation and move triumphantly through to a satisfying conclusion.

> **...if we think of this existence of the individual as a larger or smaller room, it is evident that most people only learn to know a corner of their room, a place by the window, a strip of floor on which they walk up and down.**
> **Rainer Maria Rilke**

Creative dreaming techniques such as the Senoi method offer effective tools for tackling fear whilst staying within the dream, using the imagination rather than looking for rational explanations. The dream itself remains intact; it loses none of its power, and the dreamer is able to move fully into the experience of the dream.

These techniques don't depend upon lucidity, because they can create positive dreaming patterns by the pure power of intention – to borrow a phrase from Carlos Castaneda, 'flying on the wings of intent'. However, some degree of lucidity will always come once you begin to try and exercise conscious control over your dream-life.

It may start with just a sense in the dream that you are dreaming, or the feeling that you are watching the action of the dream from above or nearby, so you are not completely identified with the dream 'I'.

Your waking 'I' becomes present in the dream like a spectator, and may make little asides. For example, I dreamt 'I was at a crystals stall, asking for "rutilated rose quartz". My waking 'I' asked, "Is there such a thing?"'

Gradually, your waking 'I' asserts itself within the dream,

sometimes even commentating and directing what happens. This is a natural development – your 'I's acclimatise.

I particularly enjoy it when someone reports a dream in which I've popped up to remind them of something. One person dreamt she put down her bag in a department store and when she turned round, it was gone. She felt very agitated, but then her waking 'I' reminded her – 'Jen says "It's your dream", so I can find my bag...' She considered going to lost property but then decided that if she thought about it very hard indeed, she could conjure up her missing bag, and that's what she did.

Another dreamer was watching a terrifying spectacle through a gap in a wall, and I suddenly appeared, chuckling. Then she remembered it was just her dream, and there was no need to be afraid.

Although you are most likely to become lucid at times when your dream 'I' is in difficult or dangerous situations, you will soon find it happening in all kinds of dreams. For example, your dream 'I' might encounter things he or she does not find odd, but your waking 'I' thinks, 'What's a kingfisher doing in an office?' If your waking 'I' doesn't like the kingfisher being in the office, she might take control and open the window.

With your waking 'I' consciously participating in your dreams, you are able to enjoy and be entertained by what your dream 'I' gets up to. Your dream 'I' becomes like a character in a story you are writing. She is 'I' in your dream, but she is not you, just as 'I' in a story is not the author. She may be your creation, but she has her own volition. You may sometimes lead, but sometimes you have to follow.

You, the dreamer or writer, have one coherent life story,

but your dream 'I' is not restricted by time or space. Your dream 'I' is more than your ego-concept of yourself; it is all the possibilities of you.

Just as your dream 'I' is much larger than your waking 'I', so the dream is much larger than the waking life. The House of Dreams is not an annexe to your waking life. It is the immeasurable context in which your waking life exists.

It can be a strange and scary place, but it can be wonderful too. Capturing dreams with the intention of interpreting them means you stay boxed up in your corner making occasional forays, grabbing images and pulling them back into your little puddle of light.

Creative dreaming techniques mean you can move fully into your House of Dreams, free from fear. You can spread out and explore. If you are used to working with dreams in a purely interpretative way you may be surprised how liberating and exhilarating that can feel.

Part Two

The House of Dreams

This part is about exploring the personal unconscious through dreaming and writing; uncovering the themes, characters, flora and fauna, and the emotional tone that characterise each person's unique inner world.

1 Making Yourself at Home

Dreams are best understood if one ceases to think of them as discreet phenomena or events but instead responds to them as momentary glimpses of the dreamer's total imaginative fabric, into which are woven all his memories, expectations, wishes and fears.

Charles Rycroft

When you first start to recall and record your dreams, you may find they're full of strange images and outrageous situations, but as you pay attention to them they begin to settle. They become less random and weird.

The first dreams one group brought to workshops included a hybrid half-piglet, half-girl; some flat, shiny, metallic insects which flashed a dazzling blue light if you stepped on one, and a dolphin with a handbag for a dorsal fin.

Within a few weeks, the weird images had gone. The dreams they brought no longer felt like strange random events, but glimpses into an inner world with its own particular character, which was both unique and consistent.

It isn't just the general quality of the settings that make the dream-world feel consistent – each person's dream-world also has its own specific places. Lots of people report having a particular house they visit from time to time in their dreams, or a place that's familiar in dreams but doesn't exist in real life.

For example, one workshop participant dreamt several times during the course about a run-down seaside town she recognised within the dream from previous dreams, although she didn't know it in waking life. Another had a familiar beach she only visited in dreams.

As well as settings, the dream-world has its own consistent history of events. A friend told me about a dream she'd had where she met a gorgeous man in a bar, and recognised him from a previous dream.

Another friend, who was fairly new to dream-working, emailed me 'to report a new type of dream where I had a dream about a previous dream I hadn't actually remembered at the time'.

He dreamt he was driving along a new stretch of dual carriageway with a colleague and he remarked that he had once lived nearby, pointing out a bit of country road he often used to drive along. He didn't recall that dream at the time, but a week later he had the identical dream again, except with a different member of staff, and then remembered within the dream that he had dreamt it before. 'I had déjà vu within the dream, recalling that I had had it about a week ago. How weird is that?'

As the dream-world settles and becomes more consistent, experienced dreamers may still encounter surreal objects and situations but they are less common; they stand out from the normal fabric of their dreams like bright jewels sewn on.

These objects are like talismans or mystical messengers – they flag up a different quality of dream, and demand a different kind of attention. But before you can see them you have to be familiar with your dream-world, so that you know what's normal and what doesn't belong there. You have to move fully into your House of Dreams, and make yourself at home.

> *I was eating strawberries and there were lots left over. Someone said, 'What shall we do with them?' and I answered, 'Once, my mother made me a jacket out of strawberries. It was very nice.'*

I loved Shetland because it felt safe, and small. It was easy to know and manage. You could learn all the seabirds and flowers in a single year of seasons. You could feel the moods of the restless sea, and lose yourself in the vastness of the sky.

You knew who lived in all the houses in your community, and what was on every shelf in every shop in Lerwick. Nobody expected or demanded anything from you; you could be as still and silent as the empty hills.

By contrast, my dream-life was busy, vibrant and full of colour, and I felt confident and proactive within it. This was an unexpected consequence of learning creative dreaming techniques to tackle the knifeman. Looking upon dreams as experience for the self meant they soon became exactly like a second life, running parallel to my waking one.

I was present in my dreams as myself, not just the dreaming 'I'. I engaged with situations, made choices and decisions, just the same as in my waking life, only free from confusion and fear.

The more I got to know my dream-world, the more aware I became that it had consistent features, like my day-world. It was characterised by certain landscapes and built environments.

My dream places were mostly parks and gardens, with

abundant flowers and leafy paths, ponds, fountains and beautiful sculptures. They often had secret summer houses and pergolas. Or they were suburban streets, like the ones I grew up in, but never city centres. The open spaces in my dream-world were beaches, mountains and bare hillsides, but never woods or fens or farmland.

My dreams were characterised by certain flora and fauna too. There were no elephants or giraffes or monkeys; no farm animals such as sheep, cows and pigs. The animals I met in my dreams were snakes, spiders, tigers and dogs; owls, swans, other birds, fishes and frogs – and these animals often had special powers. A snake might be able to turn itself into a crocodile, or a flock of tiny birds become an enormous frog. Fish might swim through the air and birds fly under the water. In my dream-world, this was normal.

There was in my dream places another kind of consistency, which didn't exist in my waking world: I came across certain shapes and numbers time and again. The numbers were '22' and '8'. They might occur separately, like the time I met 22 women on an island or the time I visited a building with the Roman numeral VIII on a brass plate on the door, but most often they appeared together.

If I entered a raffle, my ticket number would be 228. If I bought something in a dream sale, it would cost £2.28 or £228; if I stayed in a dream hotel my room would be number 228 and if I phoned someone, 228 would be the number I dialled.

The shape I noticed everywhere in my dream places was an 'L'. Buildings, flower beds and ponds were often L-shaped, and patterned areas such as paving and windows were made up of many L's. It was very curious.

Over weeks and months, I discovered that time in my dream

world worked in the same way as in the waking world. One thing followed on from another, sometimes straight away and sometimes later. One night, I saw four fat goldfish in a bowl hanging from an ornamental bridge. Other goldfish floated and swam in the air around the bowl, and one of them followed me as I went by, swimming around me in the air.

A few nights later the goldfish caught up with me when I stopped beside a pond in an ornamental garden to watch some white swans sleeping under the water. It appeared once again after that, at a party in my grandmother's house, where it chased me and bit me on the leg.

My dream world also contained its own history, so that I might remember, within a dream, something which had happened years before in a previous dream. On one occasion I dreamt 'I was eating strawberries and there were lots left over. Someone said, "What shall we do with them?" and I answered, "Once, my mother made me a jacket out of strawberries. It was very nice."'

In my dreams, my relationship with Susan continued to develop. She would sometimes be part of the action of the dream, or she might comment on things I was doing in my waking life. On one occasion she told me off for icing digestive biscuits.

'You shouldn't eat that stuff,' she said. 'It's bad for you.'

'What do you know?' I snapped back. 'You're dead!'

The dreams about Susan felt very real. The last time I saw her, I dreamt 'I was walking in a park. In front of me, on the path, there was a group of school-children, milling around. I thought I caught a glimpse of Susan in the distance, but I knew it couldn't be her because she was dead.

'The girl in the distance turned, and I saw her face really clearly. In that moment, the dream fell away, and it was real life. I was awake, and Susan was there in the bedroom looking straight at me, sitting on our bed.

'I said, "You can't be here. You're dead."

'Without a word, Susan stood up and started to walk away. I got up to go after her. She hadn't asked me to; I just did it, as I had always done.

'I followed Susan back to the park, only now everything was white – the grass, the trees, the path, the children. Susan herself was completely dressed in white and her face, when she turned to check I was still there, was white as well.

'The path through the park led to a white gate. Susan went through it with me close behind. There was a white Victorian building, which looked like our old primary school, on the other side of the road. We went through the front door, up a white staircase and along a soundless white corridor.

'Susan opened the white door that led into her room. Everything inside was white – the ceiling, the walls, the floor. The kitchen counter where we sat on high stools was white and the drink she gave me was in a white mug. I asked her, "Is it horrible being dead?"

'Susan said, no, it wasn't horrible. She wanted to stay where she was for a while and then move on to the next thing, like everyone else. But before she could move on she would have to come back and start all over again, because she hadn't seen it through.

'"This is what I came to tell you," she said. "If you kill yourself, you just have to come back and do it all again."

'We walked back down the stairs and across the road into the park. We went back to my house together and I got into bed. Everything looked normal again. Susan looked exactly as she had always looked. I couldn't take my eyes off her and yet, somehow, she disappeared without me noticing when she went.'

I had absolutely no doubt that I had seen my sister's ghost. She had come through my dream right into my room, she had woken me up; and when she had sat down on the bed we had been there together, as real and living as each other.

She had taken me, still awake, back into the dream, only it was her dream now. She had shown me her place. She had given me a message that I couldn't have come up with for myself and for that reason I was sure her visit wasn't just a dream – it had to be Susan herself.

This visitation had a very profound effect on me. I dug out my secret stash of sleeping pills and threw them in the bin. I didn't want to follow Susan any more; I had to let her go.

So my waking life moved forward, and my dreams, the two sometimes in parallel, sometimes overlapping. The more used I became to having this secret second life, the more normal it began to feel. It was the difference between falling in love, when everything is extraordinary, and being in love. It was the deepening of enchantment to commitment.

Sometimes I felt disloyal, lying in bed next to my lovely husband, watching him slide softly into sleep. I felt like a bigamist about to sneak off to my other life. But it was like an addiction, with its promise of pleasure, excitement and adventure and I could not imagine giving it up.

Most nights, at that time, I was recording five or six dreams in my diary, so it was a very strange morning indeed when all I managed to write was, 'I dreamt I was Carl Gustav Jung reincarnated.'

This dream was different in feeling tone from my usual dreams. It was also different because I didn't usually dream about public figures, especially ones I knew hardly anything about, and because I had never before started recording with the words 'I dreamt'.

I always recorded my dreams telling what happened directly – 'I went... I saw... I did'. This dream should have started, 'I was Carl Gustav Jung reincarnated', but I realised that I couldn't actually remember what it felt like being in the dream or being Carl Gustav Jung. I couldn't remember anything that had happened in the dream either – it was a dream which had no story.

Because it felt incongruous in my familiar dream-world, it made me take notice. I had never studied Jung or read anything by him, but I had bought his Memories, Dreams, Reflections in a second-hand bookshop in my late teens. I had never got around to reading it but I always intended to, and it was one of the half-dozen books I happened to have brought with me to Shetland.

I devoured Jung's memoir in a sitting. I had never personally met anyone else who had the kind of compelling dream-life I had, or the same fascination with it. But Jung didn't only go into his dream-world – he brought back what he found there and applied it to his waking life. He said that taking a scientific view of dreams was what enabled him to stay safe.

I had thought there was only one way to interpret dreams, and that was Freud's way, seeing them as dark material spewing up from the unconscious mind, which was a heaving pit of repressed urges and instincts.

Freud believed dreams were encoded into symbols in order that the conscious mind could not understand them, because otherwise the sleeper would keep waking up in horror, but an expert could crack the code by analysis.

As this had proved to be at odds with my own experience on every count, I had come to the conclusion that dreams could not be interpreted at all. But Jung proposed a completely different interpretative approach, one which made sense to me and I couldn't wait to try it.

For Jung, the unconscious wasn't full of shameful secrets you had to repress; it was everything you weren't conscious of in yourself, both positive and negative, including all your unrealised potentials. Dream symbols were the most complete expression possible for products of the mind emerging into consciousness. They were first glimpses of something you did not yet know and for that reason they were not explainable in words.

Yet they were full of meaning, meaning you could feel in your heart and in your bones, meaning you could sense in your imagination, and those were the channels you had to use if you wanted to develop understanding. Since you couldn't define what a symbol meant in any rational way you had to spend time with it, paint, play, dialogue with it, pay attention to it and allow its many-layered meanings to unfold.

Jung said the significance of dream symbols was unique to the dreamer at the moment of dreaming. They were an opening up to multiple possibilities, not a closing down to one definitive meaning, and that explained why the symbols dictionary approach hadn't worked. They were the language of poetry, and like poetry dreams required patient contemplation for the dreamer to find their own personal response.

When I had tried before to find meaning in my dreams, with the psychiatrist and the symbols dictionary, I had approached them the scientific way, dissecting them like dead frogs, cutting, rummaging, trying to find the lungs, the stomach, the heart, but a person who has never seen a living frog will not understand what a frog is by cutting up a carcass.

If you want to understand what a frog is you have to see the living frog, hopping, puffing out its throat, diving, swimming, *lying in wait for unwary flies among the reeds. You have to hear its loud unlikely sound. You have to sense the mystery of it, the magic which is the life in it.*

I had seen the frog now, I knew what it was, and Jung showed me how I might understand more without killing it off. He gave me a way of finding meaning in my dreams without ransacking and destroying them.

It made sense to me that my dream life must be linked in some way to my waking life. They were not two separate worlds because they overlapped in me. I could still wholly enter my House of Dreams, but then bring back what I found there, in order to enrich my day-world and centre myself in it again. So now, inspired by Jung, I started to listen for echoes of the day-world in my dreams.

I think every creative impulse that a working writer, or artist of any sort has, comes out of that dark old country where dreams come from.

Anne Rivers Siddons

When you first venture into your inner world as a writer, it can feel random and unfocused in the same way as your first engagement with dreams. The stories you write may feel like single events, almost accidental in nature, rather than glimpses of your total imaginative fabric.

But as you gain experience, you develop recognisable themes, landscapes, characters and scenarios. You move into and fully inhabit 'the dark old country' of your own inner world.

My children's stories have the same colours and settings as my dreams, the same themes, the same animals and

93

characters, particularly grandmothers. They have the same tone and direction, bursting through blocks, facing up to adversaries and pushing through to positive outcomes.

In dreaming-and-writing workshops you can recognise the style and character of each person's dreams in the same way you recognise their style of writing. For example, one participant's dreams and stories were very visual, with a signature motif of someone in a dull or monotone setting wearing a single bright article of clothing.

Another wrote wonderful dialogue pieces, and the dreams she brought involved detailed conversations. A third dreamt mostly about the real place she lived in, and her stories were realistic, straightforward tales of everyday life.

Dreaming and writing energise each other. They both enable you to explore your inner landscape and so become more confident within it. The great benefit of regular dream awareness for writers is that it takes you there instantly, further and deeper.

If you are not familiar with your own dream-world, you can get a glimpse of it by doing a simple collage.

Your dream-world collage

You will need:

- a bunch of old magazines, ideally including different kinds – as well as your normal favourites you could ask round your friends for their cast-offs and find freebies at your travel agent, supermarket and bank

- a large piece of paper or cardboard – it doesn't matter if it's marked or tatty because you're going to cover it
- a glue stick.

Method:

a) Start with four writing warm-ups to ease your focus into your inner world. Write for five minutes, stream-of-consciousness, from each of these prompts: 'I remember...', 'I expect...', 'I wish...' and 'I fear...'

Don't think about it – just keep your pen moving on the paper, and when one line of thought dries up, go straight on to another.

You can do this in your notebook or directly onto the piece of paper or card you're going to be using for your collage and then stick your images on top of it. If you prefer, you could write on pieces of paper and tear them up to use in your collage.

b) Spend ten minutes tearing out any image which appeals to you or provokes an emotional response. Include any patches of colour or pattern you like, as well as any words or numbers. Don't worry if you've got too many because you'll be selecting down.

c) Spend five minutes going through the images you have chosen and sticking the ones that feel right onto your paper or card. You can fill the whole surface or leave gaps, over-lap the edges or flip the card and cover the other side as well. If any are too big, tear them down to size, or over-lap them so that some are partially or wholly concealed.

Notes

The timing is important. If you allow yourself as long as you like, you lose focus and spend too long deliberating over which images to choose – your brain kicks in and overrides your instincts.

The goal is not to make art but to get a snapshot of the things that have resonance for you.

Don't use scissors – tearing helps to keep the process rapid and stops you worrying about making it 'good'.

One of my dream-world collages

Collage making is a wonderful resource that you can use at any stage in the creative process to tackle specific issues. The trick is to hold your question in the back of your mind as you flick through the magazines and tear things out. Keep it in soft focus and choose any images you fancy, without trying to rationalise whether they fit.

I use collage for creating characters, understanding the relationships between them, building settings and busting through blocks. I've used it with other published authors including Lee Weatherly, who later recommended the exercise in her book, *How to Write a Blockbuster and Get it Published*.

I like to start all my new workshop series with a collage because it's a wonderful way for everybody to physically see who is in the group. One person's collage may be full of people and faces; another person's may not include any people at all. One person may have chosen all pictures of interiors and another, all natural environments.

Sometimes someone will have one big image, which takes up almost their whole collage, and someone else will have many small images dotted across the paper with gaps in between. I've seen collages which overlap the paper in weird, extravagant ways, and others which fit exactly to the edges; collages where all the images are arranged symmetrically in rows, and others where they cluster according to colour. Once, someone made a really pretty collage, then flipped the paper over and created another one on the back that felt quite dark and sinister.

Each collage has its own unique tones and features. When we discuss them together, we consider whether there is a predominance of built or natural environments or of one element – earth, water, fire or air – over another. We look at the people and animals, and the interactions between them.

But we are absolutely clear that the intention is creative and not psychological. There is no judgement or analysis. When you make a dream-world collage, all you are doing is glimpsing the areas of experience which most spark your imagination and set up emotional resonance in you.

> **The differentiating factor is the conscious ego, which stands at the threshold of consciousness and judges the material which comes by, forms an opinion about it and makes a decision as to what is to be thought about it or done about it.**
>
> June Singer

Going over the threshold into the House of Dreams and letting the bridge burn behind you is an exciting adventure, and it gets better. As you become more familiar with your normal dream-world, you can build skills and experience lucidity.

One of the recommended techniques for experiencing dream lucidity is if you have a repeated dream – which most people do, like my knifeman – then you say to yourself before you go to sleep, 'If I dream I'm in Paddington Station (or whatever) again tonight, I'll know it's a dream.' As your whole dream-world becomes familiar, you automatically become lucid a lot of the time.

A dream task I sometimes suggest to a group is to notice an 'unexpected object' in their dreams. Some will bring a dream which does happen to contain a surprising and striking image, but others are aware of the search within the dream, thinking, 'Hmm... so what about the unexpected object?' and consciously go looking for it.

The danger is that you can become enraptured. Your dream-life can feel more exciting than the ordinary world, and you can come to identify more strongly with the multi-faceted person you are in your dreams. Even the great dream-scientists of the last century experienced something of this.

Sigmund Freud seems to have destroyed all records of his dreams except the forty-seven that he drew on for his book, *The Interpretation of Dreams*. He said, 'The stuff simply enveloped me as the sand does the Sphinx.'

Carl Jung said his dreams and fantasies would have strangled him 'like jungle creepers' if he hadn't had his family and professional life grounding him firmly in the real world.

It can happen without you noticing, this gradual shift in your centre of gravity, until you feel so much more at home in your inner world that you lose your sense of belonging in this one. My dreams didn't feel engulfing or strangling – they felt freeing and enabling. I had been happily disappearing into them, when Jung came along and pulled me back.

You can cross the threshold and explore your dream-world, but you have to live in the waking world, and therefore the dream must be subservient to the conscious ego.

One way of maintaining the right balance between them is by not only living the dream but also examining that experience objectively, and understanding how it is linked to your waking life.

The skill is to do so without destroying the dream.

2 Echoes and Objects

> Everything is gestation and bringing forth. To let each impression and each germ of a feeling come to completion wholly in itself, in the dark, in the inexpressible, the unconscious, beyond the reach of one's own intelligence, and await with deep humility and patience the birth-hour of a new clarity: that alone is living the artist's life.
>
> Rainer Maria Rilke

The value of regular dream-recall for writers is that it makes us aware of the continuous flow of stories and images moving through us all the time, like an underground stream.

For as long as we live, this flow can no more dry up than the blood in our veins, which means that if we feel blocked we know it can only be because we have closed our access to it, through over thinking, or anxiety, or reluctance to engage.

The value of trying to understand the meaning of dreams, for writers, is that it teaches you exactly the same attitudes of mind as you need to bring to the initial stages of writing.

First and foremost, you have to learn to be patient. Meaning may start to emerge almost immediately, or over a series of dreams, or after several months or even years.

It may take decades, like the knifeman was to do. The same applies to writing. This book, for example, has been almost twenty years in the making, while many books with shorter gestation times have sprung from me along the way.

Trying to force explanations out of dream symbols where their meaning isn't immediately obvious is like trying to force a rose to bloom before it is ready, and it's the same with stories. Like lots of authors, after my first few books were accepted for publication, I tried to push the pace. I bombarded my agent with half-baked, un-sellable stories before I settled into my stride. I stuck a note on my study wall to remind myself, 'Impatience is a form of resistance'.

The second quality you need in order to approach dream symbols and writing ideas alike, is receptiveness. You need to be able to sit back for as long as it takes, be passive, observe; you need to examine the symbol or idea from every angle, to wait quietly and watch to see what it does.

The third quality, when you are ready to engage with a dream or writing idea in a more active way, is a spirit of playfulness. Be like a little child, messing around with water or sand. Let yourself be totally absorbed. So much will reveal itself to you, by simple sifting, stirring and pouring. Everything you need to know about your dream or writing idea will come to you, in the first instance, through play.

I looked at my dreams and I saw they were all symbolic representations of my situation/thoughts/concerns in waking life. They were the stories underneath. They didn't explain life, they told it in a different way, a way full of possibilities rather than definitions. This seemed like an important discovery.

Looking back through my dream-diaries to see how my dreams might relate to what had been happening in my waking life, I couldn't believe I had never noticed before that they were often simple story-versions of day-time situations and events.

After a discussion with my psychiatrist about stopping therapy, for example, I had dreamt I was at university and he was my lecturer. I was telling him that I didn't want to be a student any more. Two cameramen came to set up a historical film and the psychiatrist went out into the corridor to talk to them. I tried to slip out as well, and get on with my dream somewhere else, because I felt the film had nothing to do with me, but the psychiatrist told me off.

On another occasion, after an argument with my husband, I dreamt the two of us were rowing together on a choppy river, but it wasn't fun because we were both in a bad mood. Then a big storm blew up and we clung to the sides of the boat in terror, but the wind and waves were too strong and we fell out.

It was in reading them again that I noticed my dreams were full of puns, which were another clue as to how they related to events in my day-world. If I was in any doubt that my rowing dream was about the row I had had with my husband, the puns pointed to a definite link - we went 'rowing' together and then we 'fell out.' The next day we made up, and that night I found myself walking with him in a wonderful mountainous place where we climbed up Ben More and Ben Hope.

Something else I noticed on rereading my dream diaries was that certain dream scenes seemed to crop up in response to specific situations in my waking life. Whenever I had to make a decision about something, I always dreamt I was shopping, and it seemed the bigger the decision, the bigger the shop.

After sex, I often dreamt about swimming, and the water

seemed to reflect the emotional quality of the particular sexual experience, a limpid pool with sunlight sparkling on the surface, a clear rushing river, a dangerous dark sea.

After days when I had been thinking a lot about dreams and feeling a dawning of new understanding, I would dream I was in a huge, dilapidated old house. It was a house with many rooms, but I only lived in some of them. Each time I had this dream, I opened a new door and found a room I hadn't even known was there before.

When it came to the objects in my dreams, as well as the ones that occurred frequently all the time, such as potted plants and flowers, cats, dogs and certain people I knew, I noticed that others would come in spates, so I might have a week or two with lots of dreams about badminton, or planes, or a particular person from real life popping in and hanging around for a while like a holiday house guest, then going away again.

I considered these objects in the light of what I had learned from Jung, which was that symbols did not have universal meanings like signs, but were unique and personal. My rose, for example, was not about romance, or heraldry, or religion, or any of the other suggested meanings in the symbols dictionary – the smell of an old-fashioned rose, the loose, dusky petals, always took me powerfully back to childhood Saturdays in my grandmother's garden, with its three rose bushes in the middle of a small square of grass.

The meaning of symbols wasn't fixed within the individual either, but changed according to the circumstances like a chameleon changing colour. A blank sheet of paper in one dream made me feel panicked, like I had in waking-life when I had failed to write anything at all in my mock final exams. In another dream, a blank sheet made me feel excited, like I did every morning when I opened my diary to write down my dreams.

Meaning could also steadily evolve over time. Dogs, in my early dreams, were often cowed and pathetic, and I felt sorry for them; later, they were rabid and frightening; then they were magical shape-shifters, changing from dog to cat. For a time, dogs were pushed out completely by cats. The cats had kittens, and the kittens shape-shifted into babies.

Jung said the key to meaning was through 'the bridge of the emotions'. Checking dream contents in the context of how you were feeling during the day could often light up the links of meaning between them.

I found this often happened, but if it didn't, I would never force it. I would hold the dream in my mind for a while to see if anything developed. Usually, it distilled down into one or two bright items over time.

In one such dream, 'I was with my best friend in Shetland, Anne. We were sitting on a blanket in her garden. It was a sunny day and we were drinking home-made lemonade, just the two of us, and eating egg-and-cress sandwiches. In a conversational kind of way, Anne said, "In a minute, a big bee will land on my chin. It will sting me and then I'll die."

'I jumped up, in a panic. "We've got to get inside! Hurry, before it comes!" I tugged at her arm but she stayed where she was.

'Anne looked into my eyes.

'"You don't understand," she said. "What will happen has happened."'

'What will happen, has happened' – those words were the bright items that stayed with me. They wouldn't go, and neither would the bee which came and landed on her chin straight after, big as a fist.

I found that dreams were like poems for me – I could be intrigued by an image or idea even if the rest of the poem was impenetrable and, like poems, my dreams came in all shapes and styles, from straight-talking, street-talking, easy and direct, to the mysteries of TS Eliot's Four Quartets.

If my dreams were mysterious I looked at them from every angle but then I let them be. I felt as if my dreams were always one step ahead. They were doorways into something I could not yet understand in words.

It didn't matter if I couldn't understand them yet; knowing they were connected in some way with my waking life was enough. It helped me not to get lost in them.

Intrigued by this shadowy relationship between my dreams and waking life, I started recording a few lines about what had happened during the daytime in my dream diary. Not that I had much to report. Since stopping therapy, all I really did was a part-time job monitoring local radio news for a couple of hours a day, long walks, trips to the library and visits to Anne.

It gradually occurred to me that my dreams had all the features of fiction. They had narrative strands, characters and settings; they had scenes which built to drama, terror, humour, poignancy. I started to think about writing a novel.

I had spent one sixth-form summer writing a novel, and later at university I had written another in one of my vacations, so I knew what it involved and I knew I could do it, that long immersion in another life, although I had never tried to have anything published.

Here I was now, living on a remote island, with no qualifications except a bunch of A-levels and a degree, which hadn't made the world my oyster at all, except the narrow world of education, where I knew for certain that I did not want to be.

Some people managed to make a career writing books – why shouldn't that be me? So for the next year or so, I took to walking up the peat track behind our house first thing every morning, pondering what was going to happen in my next chapter, and then going home to write it up.

I called my novel Royal Jelly. *It was weird and dreamlike, as were the pictures I drew to illustrate it. Of the six publishers I sent the first few chapters to, four asked to see the complete manuscript.*

Weird and dreamlike – Royal Jelly

But none of them took it on. They said it was 'too experimental'. I was devastated. I didn't even notice the very positive feedback that each one took the time to give me – all I saw was the rejection. I had spent a whole year working on my novel and it was as good as I could make it; if it wasn't good enough, then neither was I.

My dreams had given me access to an amazing abundance of material, but I didn't have the creative skills to control it.

There's a strange combination in writing of using images and fragments from actual dreams, but also finding a way to have a governed conscious dream life, which is what writing is. It's to have access to your own unconscious but also to direct it.

Allan Gurganus

If you have ever tried to write a poem or short story directly from a dream, you will probably have come to the conclusion that it doesn't really work. Dreams are pure subjective substance, which has to be transmuted into something a reader can share.

But although you can rarely use a dream exactly as it is in writing, dreams can be a great source of inspiration. They can energise your writing because they are fired by the very themes and emotions which are bubbling beneath the surface in your waking life.

Using dreams to spark creative writing not only guarantees you will find stories which feel enjoyable and meaningful to you, it is also a good way of deepening your understanding of the dream.

Like creative dreaming, writing stories from dream material is also a kind of rehearsal for life, a way of finding creative solutions to waking life situations, and so feeling empowered.

Here are two of the approaches I use in workshops for writing from dream material. In the first, we extract the bones of the dream and build it up into a story; in the second, we take the whole dream and distil it down.

Dream themes – building from the bones

Choose a recent dream if you would like to try this exercise because it will have more immediate resonance for you than one you had a while ago. It doesn't need to be long or detailed. All you're looking for is a moment of action.

Describe the dream in a single sentence beginning, 'Someone ...' For example, in my bee dream, I might say, 'Someone is giving a warning' or 'Someone wants to run away'.

Use non-specific nouns, 'something', 'someone', 'somewhere', if you can. Keep it as general as possible, with the focus on the verb. In my rowing dream, 'Someone is cross with her husband' would be too specific. 'Someone is cross with someone' is the pure action, plain and simple, capable of supporting a whole new cast of characters.

Other examples from workshops include, 'Someone is searching for someone', 'Someone has forgotten something', 'Someone is asking questions' and 'Someone isn't what they seem'. You get the idea.

Write a few alternative verb-focused sentences for your dream, and then decide which one you're going with. Don't over-think it. You're just playing about with some ideas.

Now forget the dream, take the sentence and build a new context around it. If your sentence is, 'Someone is being chased', who is it? Who is being chased? Start by making a character sketch.

When you are creating a character, it helps to know

their name, even if you aren't going to mention it. Be aware of the automatic assumptions you and your reader will have from your choice of name.

If I give a group of writers a list of names and ask them to jot down their first impressions of what the characters might be like, most of them will come up with the same kind of age, work and personality for each one. Feel it in yourself if I give you, for example, Sky Wychwood, Seth Braithwaite, Jane Smith, Hugo Asquith, Lyra Hart...

When you're thinking about your character's appearance, imagine you're watching a video of them, or looking through their photo album.

Then ask them a few questions to get to know them a bit. What do they like? What do they hate? What is their earliest memory? What was their childhood ambition? Ask as many questions as you need. Ask the things that you want to know.

You won't use everything you know about your characters in any story, but knowing a lot about them gives you context; it makes the writing flow more easily, and feel more three-dimensional. A story is like an iceberg; the bit the author shows you is just the tip of what they know.

Make character sketches for anyone else involved in the story – who is chasing them? Who gets in the way? Who helps them?

When you've got some good character sketches, think about the settings. Ask 'Where?' Look around at the scenery. Use all your senses to be right there. Where are they running to? Where are they running from? Ask

'When?' The season, weather, time of day and the historical era, are all part of the setting.

Then ask 'Why?' Why are they being chased? Ask 'What is the issue? What is at stake? What happens if they don't get away?'

Who, what, where, when, why, how... these are the prompts for imaginative play, and they will always take you straight into a story.

Fully imagine the scene, and when you are ready, write it. Don't try to write well, just write. It's a first draft. At this stage, being 'good' is not important. What you need is to be present.

Dream images – distilling it down

In this exercise, rather than stripping a dream to the action and building a new story around it, we start with a whole dream and reduce it down to a telling image, insight or moment in poetry.

You don't need any special knowledge of rhyme and metre in order to make a poem. What we're going for here is free verse, where the poem is defined by the succinctness of the idea, its musicality, its feeling-tone and the way it looks on the page.

Choose a dream from your diary and start by rewriting it, laying it out as a poem. Do this in a free way, using your instincts about where to put line breaks, not changing the wording at all. Don't skip this bit, because the act of rewriting is a sort of contemplation on the dream.

As you write notice:

- where is the energy of the poem for you?
- which images would you like to build?
- which parts don't really engage you?

When you have finished writing it out, trim away anything you don't need and read through it again, making notes on:

- what kind of poem is it – story, idea, description...?
- what is the voice of the poem – dramatic, humorous, confessional, lyrical, conversational...?
- does the poem trigger any interesting general thoughts or observations?

Now work your poem up, using as much or as little of the original as you like. Avoid the temptation to nail it down with rhyme and metre.

Here's an example of how this might work, from a dream I had recently. First, I rewrote it verbatim, setting it out like a poem.

A beautiful shop has opened up
Selling hand-painted pictures and artefacts
And lovingly restored old items
There's a mug, hand-painted, with an oak tree on it

In rain on one side, and sunshine on the other
I think I will buy it for (my friend).
The idea is that a strong, healthy tree
Needs bright times and rainy times to grow
It's only twenty pounds.
The tea chest it's standing on is two hundred pounds
Next door to this shop now, an ugly chavvy shop
Is opening, with loud harsh music
It will take trade from the beautiful shop
But the owner will hang in there
Though you can see he's sad

The energy of this poem for me is the idea of sunshine and rain, and the image that calls to me is the hand-painted cup. So I can cut the whole second half, from 'the tea chest'.

In passing, the bit about the two shops does reflect a choice I was thinking about at the time of the dream – I still dream about shopping whenever I'm pondering a decision.

The choice was about this book – should I dumb it down and stick to the kind of thing readers might expect from a book about dreams? Or could I do it the way I wanted to, exploring the beautiful objects of my own and other people's dream-lives, with hand-painted pictures and 'lovingly restored old items'? I went for the latter, though I felt sad to think that it would probably sell much better if it was more mainstream.

So returning to my dream-poem, I wanted to focus on the cup. I started by fully visualising it. The friend in my dream was having a hard time after the break-up of a long relationship, and she kept apologising for pouring her heart out to me.

In a beautiful shop
a handmade cup
solid and stubby
as a stump
its oak-tree half in rain
and half in dappled sun

In the kitchen my friend
tears open the tissue
soft rustle of leaves
as I make the tea

Your poem need not stay this close to the dream. Sometimes, your train of thought may take you right away from the dream. Follow it, like a fox tracking a hare. Let the image or idea take you where it wants you to go. The scenery may change completely, but the hare is still the same.

Don't try to analyse what draws you to specific objects in your dream, or what they mean. Be open to their possibilities yourself, and allow your reader to find their own resonances in them.

> Western education predisposes us to think of knowledge in terms of factual information, information that can be structured and passed on through books, lectures and programmed courses... By contrast, within the Indigenous world, the act of coming to know something involves a personal transformation.
>
> F David Peat

Listening for the echoes of your day-life in your dreams helps you to stay centred in the waking world. It grounds you, when otherwise you might become enchanted and lose yourself in the dream.

It teaches you attitudes of patience, receptiveness and playful experimentation, which are the very attitudes you need to develop in yourself for the early stages of any creative undertaking.

But before you can start, you need to see the living frog, that is to say, experience the dream without any interpretative agenda, to simply observe, so that you know what it is and understand its terms.

Your dream will yield up its meanings, but not in the same way as we in the West expect to learn. It isn't instant and definitive, like learning the names of the countries in Europe or the properties of an equilateral triangle. It's a process of coming-to-knowing, or rather coming-towards-knowing, because there is no ending, no right answer.

You have to be still and listen for echoes, dream stories which have the same themes or emotions as your day-world in the moment. You have to consider the objects of your dreams without seeking to reduce them to definitions, but simply paying attention to them.

This kind of learning is not a closing down to a single answer, but an opening up to resonances and ramifications. It will change you. Where creative dreaming such as the Senoi approach is designed to make life better, working with dreams in this way makes life bigger.

Embracing what you don't yet know, but can only sense and imagine, creates movement and opens you to the bigger picture, whereas only accepting things that can be proven fixes you, and keeps life small.

Learning from dreams in this way is like creative writing, where you explore the endless possibilities of yourself through characters and circumstances which at first might seem to have little to do with your waking life.

But you do have to treat dream interpretation with some caution. As you begin to find unmistakable echoes of your day-life in your dreams, it's easy to assume those echoes must be the essence of all of them if you could only find it.

All dreams are not the same. Some dreams go wider and deeper than the personal unconscious, and some come from places even further out, beyond human understanding.

If you wake up thinking, 'I know what that was about!' then you probably do, like my friend who finished with her boyfriend and emailed me next day, 'Woke up with one of those lovely literal dream images – I was removing the dead wood from a bush!'

If meaning emerges through gentle contemplation with the same sense of recognition, that's probably on the money too, but if there's no obvious link with the day-world, worrying away at it could lead to misunderstanding and distortion.

I think of dreams that relate to your day-to-day life as 'close-in' dreams, but it's hard to identify which ones those are until you know the whole territory of dreaming. One way of getting more 'close-in' dreams and of being sure that's what they are, is by simply asking for them.

When you ask for a dream, your dream will answer back.

3 The Voice of the Dream

> Decide specifically what you want to dream about;
> intend to dream about it.
>
> Patricia Garfield

Your dream is like a person sitting next to you on the bus journey through life. If you choose to ignore them and look straight ahead, you probably won't even know what they look like, let alone what they have to say.

But as soon as you show an interest, they will talk to you. They will reveal something of themselves, and the more you pay attention, the more they will talk. Pretty soon, dream images will start explaining themselves to you within the dream.

My daughter, at about eight or nine years old, dreamt she was in a car with a big brown bear, who said, 'I'm Granny, you know!' Patricia Garfield writes that she sometimes dreamt about an old school friend, who said to her in one dream, 'Do you know that I always represent sex to you?' I had a dream about lions and serpents which helpfully explained, 'lions for strength and serpents for intuition'.

But you don't just have to listen. If you don't know what a dream image means, you can ask. You can enter into a dialogue with your dream. You do this in exactly the same way as setting up dream-recall and tackling nightmares, through the power of intention.

During the day, think about the dream image which is mystifying you, and intend to dream about it again that night. At bedtime, run through the whole dream in your mind before you go to sleep, and ask for a dream which will expand upon it and make it clearer.

Sometimes, this will result in a series of dreams over several nights, in which the image evolves. There's a nice example of this in Robert Bosnak's *A Little Course in Dreams*, where an artist has a dream about a muddy track. The track dries out in the second dream, to be a dirt road. In subsequent dreams it becomes 'mud or clay', then an earthenware vessel and clay tiles.

Sometimes, asking will get you a direct explanation. I dreamt about a worm cast on a wall and, finding it curious, asked for another dream. The next night, I dreamt about a worm cast again, but I still felt mystified. On the third night, I dreamt about a worm cast, but this time a voice in my dream said, 'These worm casts are about leaving home...'

As well as incubating dreams to amplify and explain dream images, you can ask for dreams on a specific problem in your waking life. Say you've got a troubling physical symptom or a relationship problem or an issue at work – ask for a dream.

One time, when I was undergoing tests for a stomach problem, I asked for a dream, and this is what I got: 'I've had tests to see what's wrong with my stomach. There is a dish of tablets, some big aspirins and some serious cancer drugs. I know the pharmacist will give me the aspirins.

There's nothing really serious wrong with my stomach. It's a relief.'

Another time, I had a lump in my armpit, and while I was going through the medical thing my dream reassured me: 'You shouldn't be seeing the doctor. It's caused by all the emotional stuff that's been going on lately; you just need to talk to a friend.'

I will often ask for a dream to get ideas for my writing or workshops, or to organise my ideas if I've already got loads of material but I'm struggling to find a structure that works.

Here's a dream I had when I was pondering what topic to tackle next with a dream group, which incidentally gave me the content for a school workshop I was doing later in the week: 'I'm telling the group that dreaming for a purpose can mean you wake up not just with a dream narrative but also a solution to a problem in waking life. "For example," I tell them, "I've woken up today thinking that I can do a hero-journey visualisation with the Year Five/Six children and talk about that story-shape."'

One of the benefits of incubating dreams to address situations in waking life is that it means you know what the dream is likely to be about when you record it, even if it isn't immediately obvious. As you look for echoes, you know roughly where to find them in your day-life. It also means you will have a higher proportion of these 'close-in' dreams, which are accessible and easy to explore.

You can experiment with dream incubation in a playful way, not attached to any particular dream puzzle or waking-life problem. I asked one group to intend to dream about a tree. Four of the five people who came to the next session a week later brought tree dreams.

One, on the first night, had woken up feeling disappointed because she hadn't dreamt about a tree. But on the second night she dreamt about a sapling on a chalky hillside; on the third, a thin tree, and on the fourth a group of saplings. She was quite pleased, but would have liked to dream about some full-size trees.

The second person, not getting a tree dream on the first night, wrote a poem about a tree as a way of focusing her intention. Then she dreamt about a ranch with horses, and alongside it, a tree which looked like a child's drawing of a tree. Later in the dream, she thought, 'There was a tree!'

The third person also wrote down her intention to dream about a tree and was excited to wake from a dream about two young trees she had recently planted. The fourth dreamt about saplings too.

Maybe they dreamt about young trees and saplings because they were new to the idea of dream-incubation. Maybe if I'd repeated the exercise a few weeks later, they'd all have dreamt about mighty oaks!

Sometimes, you barely even need to register your intention. One of the people in that group mentioned that her husband frequently dreamt about flying, and she felt quite jealous. 'I wish I could have dreams like that,' she said. In her dreams, her feet were always firmly on the ground.

The next week, she told us she had had an amazing dream in which she was floating weightlessly above the beach at Durdle Door, then gradually gliding down past topaz-coloured cliffs and landing softly on the sand three hundred feet below.

Patricia Garfield quotes one research finding that the median time for a self-suggested dream to appear is five weeks, although some people can begin reliable dream-incubation within a fortnight.

I first tried to do dream-incubation with the tree group after only a few weeks, suggesting they intend to dream about a horse, but it didn't really work. We had been working together for eight weeks before I tried again with trees.

So if you want to experiment with these techniques, don't give up too quickly. Persevere. It will be worth the effort.

I saw a cake with one candle on it, and a little baby girl, and the voice in the dream said she was mine.

One of the things I loved about my husband was that he thought writing books was a proper job, and he totally believed I could do it. It wasn't as if we moved in literary circles; neither of us had ever even met an author before.

But he was really the only person who took my writing ambitions seriously, and a number of our friends actually told me they thought my writing was a kind of work-avoidance strategy.

So it was really hard when Royal Jelly was rejected. I felt foolish ever to have thought that I could be an author, let alone to have wasted so much time and passion working on something which had turned out to be worthless.

I went to the job centre; it felt as if I didn't have any choice. There was plenty of work in Shetland at that time, because of the oil. There were office jobs in the council and private businesses that I could apply for, and at least I would be earning more money if I had a full-time job. That night I had a dream.

I dreamt 'I was filling out an application form for a job in the Planning Department. All the people who had already filled in their applications were there, but the boss came out and told me he was offering me the job, on account of my obvious form-filling skills.

'I accepted, envisaging a car, money, a role in society. But then a friend said, "Do you actually want to dress up smart every morning? Do you want to run around making coffee for the boss? Do you seriously want to be like her?" He nodded towards the secretary who was bustling round the Job Centre offices, subservient and eager to please. I knew I didn't.'

The dream seemed very direct and clear. Indeed, since I had started looking for echoes of my day-world in my dreams, they seemed to have become easier and easier to spot, and their meaning more and more obvious.

I still had the radio-monitoring job, and I decided to try to supplement that with some cottage crafts such as knitting and papier mâché. While I was learning craft-making skills, I kept having dreams about writing and, gradually, the way I was thinking about it started to change.

In one dream, I was sending the manuscript of Royal Jelly to a publisher. I stuck stamps on the package and then on the self-addressed return envelope inside. In doing so, I noticed I had made a stupid mistake – I had put the publisher's address on the sae and my own on the outside.

I understood this dream to mean that I had written Royal Jelly for myself, and if it wasn't publishable, that was because

I hadn't aimed it at publishers or considered how it might fit into the market.

By way of confirmation, I then had a dream in which a voice said that although my book was not sale-able, that did not mean I wasn't saleable as an author.

In the last dream in this series, I dreamt 'I was working in a small craft-makers' co-operative, putting together macramé hangings from a set pattern and making beads on a bead machine. At coffee-time, someone said, "Why don't you do something more creative than this? You could, you know."

'The boss said, "Yes, it's a pity you didn't finish your book."

'"I did finish it," I said.

'Someone else said, "She might get it published with a different publisher."

'"I'll look into that for you," said the boss. "You sit down and write another one."'

It felt as if my dreams were telling me what to do, and my husband thought I should try to write another novel too, so I started to plan. This time, I thought in terms of the market, and decided my next book would be a murder mystery.

I hadn't got much beyond creating the characters and plotting the big scenes when I had a dream which unsettled everything. There was a child's birthday party happening in our living room. I saw a cake with one candle on it, and a little baby girl, and the voice in the dream said she was mine.

I had never given a moment's thought to having children, but suddenly the idea seemed to move in and set up home in me. It rattled around and made a lot of noise. Everyone said my body clock must finally be kicking in. I was twenty-seven, which was considered late for a first pregnancy in 1979.

In those days, you had to wait at least six weeks after your last period before you could take a test to find out whether you were pregnant, but I was impatient. As soon as we started trying for a baby, I asked for dreams.

I had read in Patricia Garfield that you could incubate a dream with the specific intention of gaining information and it stood to reason that my unconscious mind must know everything that was going on in every cell of my body. So each night, before I went to sleep, I asked, 'Am I pregnant?'

On 25th November, I dreamt I was holding a cardboard dial in my hand. It was a pregnancy tester. The next day, I dreamt I was a few weeks pregnant, but as we'd only been trying for a few weeks I didn't know if I could believe it.

A week later, I was still asking the question and I dreamt 'Hope came to the door, with her long hair tucked into her belt. She said she had come to congratulate us "for all the love you've got going in here". What did she mean? She nodded towards the living room. She meant the new baby. I didn't know whether to ask her in or not.'

At the end of December I had a pregnancy test which was positive. My estimated due date was 22nd August, meaning I must have conceived around 16th November. It seemed my dream really did know what was going on in my body before I did, and what's more it was happy to oblige with answers if I had any questions about it.

For the next six months or so, I had lots of dreams about the baby and the birth, but they were mostly so weird and random, I didn't try to understand them at all. Then I suddenly had a week of dreams which had a quite different quality to them.

They felt direct, understandable, and urgent too, because they seemed to suggest that the pregnancy was unstable. In mid February I dreamt I had a pain, went to the toilet and pale pink stuff came out. I told my husband it felt like a warning. In the dream, we were both really worried.

We were on a train to London, en route for an Easter break in Paris, when I went to the loo and pale pink stuff came out. We got off at York, where a doctor diagnosed a threatened miscarriage. After a week's bed-rest, things had settled down, and we headed home.

That summer was warm, for Shetland. We went camping on the beach with friends in early July. I slipped and fell on wet grass, and although nothing happened straight away I did wonder if that could have been what caused my waters to break a week later.

It was six weeks before my due date. We didn't realise that was a big problem until we got to hospital in Lerwick and the doctor put us straight on the air ambulance to Aberdeen. He said the baby would definitely need to go into a special care baby unit as soon as it was born, and we could only hope I didn't go into labour before we got there.

There was no room in the back of the air ambulance for my husband. He sat at the front with the pilot, while I lay in the back with the midwife on a narrow seat beside me, holding her hand on my belly to check for contractions.

A young doctor perched at the end near my feet, fretting and chewing his nails. There wasn't really any need to tell us, but he did anyway, many times, that he had never delivered a baby before. 'She's not in labour, is she?' he kept asking the midwife. 'Tell me she isn't in labour!'

I still wasn't in labour when we arrived at the hospital, and they gave me an injection to prevent it from starting. They said even a few more days would help the baby, but they would have to monitor me closely because once the waters had broken there was a high risk of infection.

Other women came in, had their babies, and went home. The infection set in on the third day. My temperature rocketed. I was rushed down to the labour ward and induced. I didn't even see my baby when she was born, because they bundled her up and took her straight to the special-care baby unit. I was bereft.

The first time I saw my baby, she was in an incubator. She was very tiny. Her eyes were tight shut, her skin was like paper, and the down of dark hair on her head had been shaved where the drip went in.

Later, they took the drip away and fed her milk through a tube into her nose, and later still they let me put her to the breast. Finally, after ten days, we were allowed to take her home.

Neither of us had any experience of babies, and our families were 750 miles away. Our friends gave us lots of advice, but while some were adamant that the new Penelope Leach approach was the only way to go, others with older children still favoured Dr Spock.

I listened to the advice and got the books, but if in doubt, I fell back on my dreams. For example, when the baby was three months old, some of our friends thought we should move her through into her own room. But I felt she was still too small. She was three months old but really only six weeks, if you counted from her due date. I asked for a dream.

I dreamt 'I was lying in a double bed with a couple, and a baby was in her cot alongside. The health visitor came, snatched the baby up and examined her. She took the baby off into another room, where a fat nurse wrapped her up and put her in a cot.

'"She's cold," I said. "You can't put her in here."

'"It's time for her to come in here, and come in here she must. She'll soon learn!" said the health visitor.

'"She will not," I said, and took her back to our bedroom.'

I had similarly direct dreams when it came to weaning my baby. I asked for a dream about the timing, and also about which foods would be best to start with. I asked for dreams about all the things that other women seemed to know instinctively.

Obviously, I didn't follow the voice of the dream slavishly. I trusted it insofar as I knew it was the voice of my own intuition, but I weighed everything in the balance when it came to making decisions.

I was grateful to have my dreams to guide me, but I kept them to myself. It didn't seem like the kind of thing other people might understand.

I think we all carry our own talismans and our own magical objects with us, so a book of dream symbols would do me no good whatsoever. What's important is learning your own personal vocabulary.

Sue Grafton

When you enter into a dialogue with your dreams they will often answer your questions in a direct and obvious way, but if they don't, you can re-enter the dream awake, by dialoguing with its individual symbols.

Everybody's inner world is characterised by its own scenery, people, flora and fauna, a personal treasure trove of magical objects we carry with us all the time. We can deepen our understanding of ourselves through exploring the imaginal and emotional ties that bind us to, say, owls in general; we can understand our current situation by engaging with the particular owl that was in our dream last night.

This is not a job for the rational mind. Word association games can help you move into the subjective, symbolic way of thinking.

Symbolic thinking – getting in the zone

Next to each of the following nouns, write the first word that comes into your mind, for example:

monkey... *playful*

teapot... *comforting; Bournemouth*

Do it quickly, without censoring yourself, even if you find yourself sliding straight into stereotypes. If two words come up at once, write them both. If nothing comes up, move on to the next word.

camera...	Ferrari...
oak tree...	church...
ocean...	Finland...
cactus...	doctor...
daffodil...	ear...
ginger beer...	elephant...
bells...	moon...
pullover...	tiger...

Now find some of your personal symbols for human qualities by writing the first concrete object or objects that come to mind in response to this list of adjectives, for example:

| joyful… | *beach ball* |
| intelligent… | *book, spectacles* |

curious…	angry…
lucky…	hard-working…
contented…	depressed…
sexy…	competitive…
adventurous…	grieving…
wise…	forgetful…

Finally, list ten people you know, a mix of family members, colleagues, neighbours and friends. Next to each name, write the first object or objects that come into your mind. Don't censor – and destroy after writing!

This is harder because people are complex and the better you know someone the more difficult it is to find one satisfying image. So it's more important than ever not to think about it. Just write.

For example:

| Uncle Clive… | *piano, toffees* |
| Mrs Tring… | *twig* |

When you've done that, forget about the person for a moment and jot down some of the associations you have with these objects. You may find that your image captures the person you know surprisingly well:

Uncle Clive...   *piano - music, entertainment, polish, practice*
toffees - sweet, comforting, old-fashioned
Mrs Tring...   *twig - thin, snappy, dry, alert (when you 'twig' what's going on)*

The best way I have found for opening a dialogue with a symbol is by drawing or painting it, because when you have an actual image in front of you it's easier to focus on the thing itself and not get sidetracked into interpretative ideas about what it might mean.

The process of drawing and painting is also an effective way of disengaging the critical mind for a while and allowing the playful, creative mind to move centre-stage. This makes it a good tool for starting a writing session, either in a group or on your own.

Here is an exercise I use for dialoguing with symbols, both as a dreamer to deepen my understanding of my own dreams and as a facilitator helping writers to develop dynamic characters.

Dialoguing with a symbol

You will need:

A sheet of unlined paper

A pen or pencil

Coloured felt-tips, pastels or paints (optional)

a) Choosing the symbol

Look through your recent dreams and find an image you would like to explore. Don't over-think it – go with your instincts.

If you haven't recorded any dreams recently but you are currently thinking about or working on a piece of writing, choose one of your characters and write down the first concrete object that comes into your head when you think about him/her.

If you haven't got any recent dreams or writing-in-progress, enter your inner space by closing your eyes and taking a few slow, easy breaths. Ask for an image to come into your mind. Go with the first thing that comes, whatever it may be.

b) Drawing the symbol

If you feel inhibited, remember the point of this isn't to make art, but to conduct an investigation. It doesn't have to be good; it just has to serve its purpose. If you still feel inhibited, try drawing with your non-dominant hand. That gets the idea of 'good' and 'bad' right out of the way.

When you have drawn your image, fill in the background. It doesn't have to be the same as in your dream or piece of writing. Ask the image, 'Where would you like to be? What would you like on your left...?' and so on, until you feel the picture is complete.

If you enjoy painting or working with pastels, colour it in. As well as meaning you get to spend longer with the image, colouring can key you in to the emotional tone. Painting red onto a piece of paper gives a rush of energy; blue is restful; green is nurturing; yellow is friendly. Or of course, in your specific picture red could feel like anger; blue like decay; green like nausea and yellow, barren like a desert. Whatever the feeling in the dream or writing, it will come back to you intensely in painting.

c) Starting a dialogue

When you have finished drawing or painting your image, ask some questions. What are you doing in my dream/writing? What do you want? Ask any who, what, where, when, why, how questions that come into your head. Be aware that by now you may have a fair idea about what the image 'means', and make sure you put it to one side. Dialogue directly with the image.

Remember you aren't looking for a rational explanation. You are looking to deepen your understanding of the image through experiencing it, the same way that we come to knowing in real life.

Dialoguing with dream images is another way of hearing the voice of the dream.

> If we see compensation as part of our consideration of the dream when we're awake, we're less likely to get involved in attributing God-like powers to the 'unconscious mind'.
>
> Joe Friedman

When you enter into a dialogue with your dreams by asking for information, you will begin to hear the voice of the dream, either in much clearer echoes and images, whose meaning seems obvious, or as an actual commentary within the dream.

The voice of the dream will often affirm something you were thinking or planning, or challenge decisions you might then choose to re-examine. It can feel like a wise voice, and it might be tempting to treat it as some kind of oracle. But this would be a mistake.

When it comes to asking for advice about waking life in close-in dreams, the voice expresses your personal unconscious, which contains all the memories you've lost, thoughts and ideas you haven't acted upon, things around you of which you're only subliminally aware. It comes from instincts which may have become distorted or disguised by over-thinking or anxiety.

When I asked for advice about working in an office or being a writer, it was the voice of my deepest desire, which at that time was crushed almost out of existence. When I asked for advice about weaning my baby, it was the voice of my maternal instinct, which I wasn't confident in and needed to have confirmed.

The voice of the dream, when you are asking for insight into a waking-life situation, doesn't come from a source of wisdom outside the self, or even the highest wisdom within the self – it comes from aspects of the self which are currently undiscovered, neglected or suppressed.

What the voice of the dream can offer you – and this is a very precious gift – is a wider perspective on a waking-life situation, bringing into awareness everything you believe, feel or know on an unconscious level. It can help you make sound, informed decisions, but you should not let it make decisions for you.

Listen to the voice of your dream, weigh up what it has to say, and then make up your waking mind what you want to do about it. Treat your dream like a friend who knows you well and has your best interests at heart, but may not always give you advice you want to follow.

If the voice is confused or unclear, you can get closer to it by dialoguing with the images. Eighteen months after my first child was born, and pregnant again, we were having to make some decisions about our future, and I started to dream about shopping.

I drew a picture, beginning with the words, 'Going Shopping'. First, I drew my face, then the horizon. I realised I was in water, or 'all at sea'. On the horizon, I put an island, to represent Shetland, and a setting sun, with the words, 'Island sunset'. I noticed the pun, and made the island into an eye.

'Island Sunset'

By the time I had painted the picture I knew that, although I had no idea where I was going (there was no other land in it at all), my time in Shetland was coming to a close. It had been a period of contemplation and self-discovery. Now I was ready to go south again.

This was a moment of resolution, not an oracle. It was the culmination of months of wondering whether or not to stay in Shetland, which we still absolutely loved, but where my husband's career prospects would be limited and our children would be growing up far away from their extended family.

After we left, I stopped recording my dreams for eight

years, and when I came back to it I was in a completely new place. My dream said, 'You have visited the islands of body, heart and mind, and you have come to the island of spirit...'

Part Three

The Landscape Beyond

This part looks at the mythic dimension or collective unconscious, the various layers of group and universal human consciousness we can tap into in dreams and creative writing.

1 Where Dreamers Meet

Of the universal mind each individual man is one more incarnation. All its properties consist in him.

Ralph Waldo Emerson

When you have been recording your dreams for a while, you gradually come to realise that you are not alone. The echoes and objects you find in your dreams are not confined to your own personal experience. You pick up things from other people's dreams and day-worlds too.

In a dream group, there's a definite tendency for people to dream about the same themes and images at the same time, even when we don't set up a group intention.

For example, six weeks into one group, two people brought dreams about hospitals, and two about drains. We normally bring one dream each to share, but quite often someone will remark, upon hearing another person's dream, 'One of my other dreams this week included a man in a wheelchair/ group of women in an underground chamber/ wedding ceremony too!'

These shared images can be unusual and specific, such as the time someone brought a dream about a farm which had dozens of wooden cabins the size of phone-boxes in the courtyard, painted turquoise; the dream I had brought to the session was about a school which had dozens of child-sized wooden houses in the playground, painted pink.

Another interesting thing, which happens in a group or family situation, is that one person might dream about another's waking life. My grown-up daughter phoned to tell me a dream she had had in which I was dancing to folk music in a circle of women. She thought it was funny because it wasn't the kind of thing I usually did, but it just so happened that I had done it the previous evening.

A few years ago, I dreamt my mother was showing me round a house she was planning to buy. The next time she phoned, I asked her if anything exciting was going on in her life and she said, 'Well yes – I'm thinking of moving.' It was the first I had heard about it, but she had already found a house she liked, and I asked her to describe it to me.

The striking thing about the house I had dreamt was that there was a long, narrow garden building with a living room at the end. The house she had seen – and now lives in – had just such a building; a narrow garage with a living room built on the back.

More recently, I had a dream which gave me an idea for a task I thought my dream group might find interesting, so I emailed it to them. Someone who was on holiday at the time told us she had dreamt, while she was away, that we were all sitting round my table in the group and I said, 'I'm going to go to sleep now, and dream what you will have to do.' Later that day, she picked up my email.

You can sometimes also get a kind of dream-exchange. For example, last week, I had a dream in which my younger daughter popped up quite incongruously, so I wondered what she was doing in it. I told her my dream and she said she had dreamt that night that she had come to visit me.

I heard about yet another kind of joined-up dream experience from my friend Katherine Langrish at a writers' conference. She called it 'roughs and smooths'. This is how she described it in her guest post on my *Writing in the House of Dreams* blog:

'When I was a child, I used to have a recurrent dream – or nightmare – in which I would be lying in bed, apparently awake, and see a thing like a stone or boulder come rolling from one corner of the ceiling (and yet as if from a million miles away) – and as it came, everything went *crumpled*. It would roll and roll across the ceiling, and with it came a sickening sensation as if I was seeing the skin of the world pulled off and chaos underneath. Then it would roll back again and everything would go smooth, but the feeling remained, because I knew that underneath the appearance of smoothness, the sickening crumples were still there.

'It was a dream that was often repeated, and the feeling often heralded it, so that it was possible to say to myself, *Oh, it's coming*. As I grew older the feeling would sometimes come without the dream, and after the age of about eleven or twelve, it vanished for ever.

'While I was still having them, I told my mother about them, and she said, "Oh, do you get those too? I used to have them, and so did my father; he called them *roughs and smooths*." My mother's and grandfather's versions were slightly different. I think she said my grandfather saw 'it' as something like a barrel. For herself she said, "something came towards me rolling, and everything broke up. But you stop getting them when you're about twelve." I remember feeling a mild but real relief that she knew what I was talking about.

'I never told my own children about the dream, because I didn't want them to have it, and I didn't want to suggest anything to them which might influence them into having it, but they both did get variants after all, and one daughter in particular was prone to them. Aged about seven, having woken upset, she told me, "I see squiggly lines" – she drew one in the air with a finger – "squiggly lines, and it all goes wrong." Asked next morning, she said she'd be half asleep, half awake, and see "squiggly lines, jagged lines, calm lines. They come and go. There's a horrible feeling with them."

'I reassured her that she'd simply got the family dream, and it wasn't anything to worry about, and would take itself off when she was about twelve. And it did.'

You could argue that all these things might be explained by telepathy, and it does seem that regular dream-awareness can increase a person's telepathic powers. However, there are also occasions when you dream something that you definitely have no previous knowledge about, and neither does anyone around you.

The narrator in *The Art of Dreaming* tells Don Juan a dream in which he bought an antique walking stick and the salesman told him the handle was made of iridium, which was one of the hardest substances in the world.

Don Juan asks him, 'What is iridium?' but he has no idea. He's never heard of iridium; he didn't think it was even a proper word, but when he looks it up, he finds that iridium is the second densest element known to man.

Someone at a group told us she had had a dream with no narrative, but just a word. The word was 'Thaddeus'. I asked her if she knew what it meant, and she seemed surprised at the suggestion that it might mean anything at all. No one in the group knew. We looked it up and found that Thaddeus was another name for St Jude – and his feast day was 28th October, the day she had had the dream.

On a residential workshop, someone dreamt about a train which had a picture of a little brown bird on the side and the name 'Sylvia'. He had no idea what that might mean. When I got home, I looked it up, and found that the genus 'Sylvia' is a warbler of the thrush family.

A few years ago, while house hunting, I was quite interested in a bungalow called 'Avalon'. I had a curious dream about it, in which the house looked exactly like it was in real life, except that the garden was full of coffins. I looked up 'Avalon' in my Cambridge Encyclopaedia, and found, 'In Celtic mythology, the land of the dead...'

Through dream experiences such as these, we get a growing awareness that we don't dream in isolation. The dream is bigger than our personal unconscious. Although we start inside our House of Dreams, we can gain access from there to the landscape beyond.

An old lady in a bright pink dress appeared. She had tiny legs, like a child, and looked almost deformed, but I knew she was my main helper here.

After our second child was born, we bought an L-shaped house in Cornwall with a glimpse of the sea, and there we had two more babies. It was the have-it-all eighties, but I didn't want to have it all. I wanted to stay at home and look after my children.

Fortunately, my husband agreed. Both of us had grown up in families where our mothers were the main breadwinners, at a time when that was unusual, so it was probably the inter-generational pendulum swing at work in us.

Being with small children, seeing the world through their eyes from their very first encounters with it was a magical opportunity for me, and I am intensely grateful to have had it.

Magical times

Four children meant eight years of unsettled nights and early starts, so although I still remembered lots of dreams, I didn't write them down.

I didn't write anything during that time, but I read voraciously, in quiet moments during the day and in the evening after the children had gone to bed. Mostly, I read books about psychology, including current and historical definitions of mental illness and ideas about how to cure it.

It bothered me, the notion of trying to analyse and define a human being at all, let alone through focusing down on the events of his personal past, or the chemical organisation of his brain. It didn't sit with my experience of bringing new children into the world, each one so different and so much him-or-herself. It seemed disturbing how much the assumptions of psychology underpinned our cultural understanding of ourselves and the world.

I read about dreams as well, of course, and consciousness, one book leading on from another, as I picked up the next thread from the bibliography at the back, following my curiosity. By this circuitous route I eventually reached my big reading project – the complete works of Jung.

I ordered a couple of volumes at a time from my local library, and worked my way through them, rereading some passages many times if the meaning was hard to grasp.

The thing I found most fascinating, and most confusing, was Jung's concept of the collective unconscious. This seemed to be like a reservoir of all human knowledge and experience, innate in every individual.

The collective unconscious had different layers. There was the group consciousness you shared with your family and ancestors; the wider consciousness of your country, your culture, your era, and ultimately of the whole of humanity, both right now and back to the beginning of time.

The products of the collective unconscious could theoretically emerge in an individual's dream in exactly the same way as the products of the personal unconscious. Most intriguingly, each individual's life experience and knowledge became part of the collective unconscious in its turn.

I wasn't sure if that was what Jung was saying, but I did feel clearer on his idea of the collective unconscious as a template or pattern on which all individual experience was built. His idea of archetypal events and figures made perfect sense to me.

Archetypal events were the universal aspects of life that people everywhere and at all points in history shared. They included things such as birth, death, separation from parents and marriage, which are the same for everyone at the deepest level but with huge cultural and then personal differences.

Archetypal figures, such as the mother, the baby or the wise old man, were similarly capable of endless cultural and individual variation and yet, at the deepest level, the basic template was shared by all.

Jung said the archetypes were pieces of life, not an abstract idea; you could not understand them in a theoretical way, but only through experiencing them. I began to notice and experience them in my dreams.

In the early years, my dreams had always been populated by a large but fairly stable cast of characters, like a TV soap, made up of family and friends, neighbours and acquaintances, with occasional guest appearances from famous people. The focus shifted from one group to another at different points along the way, with new characters coming in and old ones dropping out, but the vast majority were people I knew or had known in waking life.

By the time I started recording my dreams again, I was aware of characters of a different kind, who appeared with increasing frequency. I thought of them as the faceless ones. They were generic entities, with no name or personality – the helper, the manager, the muse, the baby, the old man, the old woman...

These figures had a sort of other-worldly quality, and the situations they were in felt somehow more important. For example, in one dream, a baby was floating face down in a freezing river and I was trying to save it.

'As I waded out into the rushing water, I looked up and saw an island, with a square building on it. No one lived there any more. An old lady in a bright pink dress appeared. She had tiny legs, like a child, and looked almost deformed, but I knew she was my main helper here.'

The faceless ones were often small, like undernourished children, but I knew in the dream that they would grow to normal size. Their presence in my dreams enabled me to see how they related to the other characters, and to me.

When I had first come across the idea of archetypes in Shetland, I had thought some symbols were archetypes and some weren't, and I had felt frustrated because I couldn't tell which were which. Now I began to see the archetypes as a layer of meaning from which all symbols emerged, a sort of substratum of the dream, and from there, of the waking self.

So, if I dreamt about certain people I found difficult in real life, they may simply represent themselves, but they may also carry elements of the Shadow archetype, that is to say, the opposite of my self-image. If I dreamt about my beloved senior lecturer at university she may be just herself in the dream, but she may also carry aspects of the Mother archetype, or the Crone.

If a woman dreamt about a husband or lover, he might reflect aspects of her Animus archetype, which embodied what we traditionally think of as masculine attributes, such as ambition, power and effectiveness in the world. In a man, this archetype was called the Anima, and she represented the gentle, receptive, nurturing side of his nature.

The Animus figures in my dreams came in at first as faceless ones – a man my age with long hair, an artist or musician, an outsider, an observer, a tramp. Then they came as people I knew, but with the force of the archetype. A friend with telltale tiny legs, who I knew would grow.

One night I dreamt about writing a book. The voice of the dream said, 'This is the arrival of the Animus archetype in your life...' My youngest child had just started playgroup and I knew I needed a job. I talked to a friend – one of those Shadow-bearers in my dreams, very successful in her career – and she said she thought writing books would be the perfect fit for me.

I was a person who loved having children, she said, and writing a book must be a bit like a pregnancy – the long patient months with nothing to show, while the book is growing in the secret darkness, and then the incredible birth of something new into the world.

I needed a job, but I still didn't have any useful qualifications and I was once again living in a remote area with limited work opportunities. So I decided to have another try at being an author.

As soon as I sat down to write, I had a feeling of homecoming. I felt as if this was the thing I had been born to do. I wrote a children's book in the first fortnight, then another one. After that, I did a full-length adult murder mystery and started a comic romance about aliens on holiday here on earth.

I only had two hours a day for writing, although after a few months we converted the potting shed into a plotting shed so I could go off out there to write on Saturday mornings too.

I sent my work to a handful of agents and one of them invited me up to London. She told me, on the strength of the pieces I had sent her, that I could probably be published as both a children's and an adults' writer, but I should start with children, not because that was easier but because, being shorter, children's books were usually quicker to write.

On my youngest child's last day of part-time school, I got a letter from the agent telling me officially that she would like to take me on. It so happened that Michael Morpurgo was visiting *the school that very day, and he was with the same agent.*

I plucked up my courage to talk to him, and he was very friendly towards me, but I suddenly felt overwhelmed. The idea of sitting in my plotting shed writing books was pure happiness, but the idea of being part of a world of writers, publishers and agents was terrifying.

My agent placed six children's books with publishers for me over the course of that year, including several works of fiction, a biography of Van Gogh and a retelling of Androcles and the Lion.

At the time, I was completely unaware of any link between that particular myth and the circumstances I was writing it in, but then I hadn't properly thought about myths, except in a theoretical way.

I understood that mythology contained the archetypal templates for all human experience, but I was as yet unaware of their power at work in my life.

A myth is a public dream; a dream is a private myth.
Joseph Campbell

Our experience of waking life is a construction of stories. We imagine the future in terms of stories and we organise and make sense of the past in the stories of memory. Memory is not fixed. It is less factual than it seems. It changes with new experience, so that we endlessly reframe the past, causing its characters and plotlines to grow and develop.

The template for all the stories of human experience is mythology. The archetypal events and characters are there in myths and legends of every culture, but they transcend culture to express universal truths about what it is to be human.

Take the first myth I had published, from classical culture, the story of Androcles and the Lion. The details are specific to its time – Androcles is a Roman slave who escapes from a merchant vessel in Africa; he overcomes his fear of a lion, taking pity on its pain and removing the thorn from its paw; he returns to Rome and is thrown into the arena, where he comes face-to-face with the very same lion; the lion refuses to attack him, and Androcles is given his freedom.

The details are specific but the meaning of this story is universal. It is the story of every person who has had the courage to overcome fear, and found his courage rewarded. It is my story, setting out on the adventure of being an author. It is also the story of anyone who has done someone a kindness, and been repaid.

To take an example from Christian mythology, the story of the Prodigal Son means that if a sinner returns to the church all his sins will immediately be forgiven and he will be embraced back into the fold.

But beyond that tradition, it will resonate with everyone as the story of the teenage years. The child removes himself, feeling sometimes embarrassed by his parents, sometimes angry; he keeps a growing part of his own life private from them, in order to discover who he is and create his own separate identity. When the child returns as an adult, the parents rejoice.

The story of the Prodigal Son will speak to anyone who has argued with a friend and experienced the joy of reconciliation, or made a mistake and been forgiven, or gone through any kind of transition.

In one of its earlier versions *Writing in the House of Dreams* was going to be called 'Pomegranate', in reference to the myth of Persephone. Her story could express any transition from innocence to knowledge. When you know something, you can never un-know it – you can't go back to the time before.

When you begin to explore your dream-world, it changes you. You see things in a way you didn't see them before, and you can never fully return to your old way of seeing.

In the same way, the act of writing changes you. You discover things in yourself you didn't know were there. You develop a different way of seeing and being in the world. You let the genie out of the bottle, and it becomes part of a larger you.

For that reason, when we're looking at myths in dreaming-and-writing workshops, the myth of Persephone seems an appropriate place to start. In case you are unfamiliar with it, the story goes like this.

Persephone in the Underworld

Persephone was the daughter of Demeter, the goddess of harvests. They roamed the world together making the plants grow, filling them with flowers and fruits.

Hades, the god of the Underworld, wanted to marry Persephone, but he knew Demeter would never agree to it, so he kidnapped Persephone and carried her down to his shadowy kingdom.

Demeter was distraught to find her daughter missing and she abandoned her duties to go looking for her. She left the crops to fail and the grapes to wither on the vine, and the whole world was plunged into famine.

Demeter searched everywhere for Persephone, crying and calling her name, until finally a shepherd took pity on her and told her what had happened. Demeter was furious. She went to Zeus and demanded he get Persephone back. Until then, there would be no harvests, she said, and for all she cared the entire human race could perish.

Zeus told Hades he would have to give Persephone back but Hades refused on the grounds that she had eaten six pomegranate seeds and anyone who ate the fruit of the Underworld was never allowed to return to the upper world again.

Since Persephone had eaten six seeds, Zeus decreed, she must stay in the Underworld for six months of every year, but she could spend the rest of the time in the world above with her mother.

Now, when Persephone has to go back to the Underworld, Demeter grieves. The leaves die on the trees, and the fruits drop to the ground. But when her daughter returns, they roam the world together, bringing new growth and harvest everywhere they go.

Persephone misses the sunlit fields of her mother's realm and loves coming back but she is also glad when the time comes for her to return to the Underworld because in that dark mysterious kingdom, she is queen.

When you read this story, it will resonate with particular areas of your own life. It may speak to you as a parent, or a child; as a writer, disappearing for long periods from joined-up social life into solitary realms of imagination; as a dreamer, with two lives, one at night and the other in the day-world above.

Those are a few broad-stroke ideas, but the story is capable of endless permutations. In workshops, no two stories from this myth are ever the same. Writing your own story is the best way of experiencing the myth at work in you right now.

Your Persephone myth

Start by writing a list of Persephone situations in real life. These might be as small as learning that Father Christmas isn't real, or as big as a bereavement; as particular as hearing a piece of gossip, or as general as growing up. Anything that brings new knowledge and experience from which there is no turning back because it changes how you see yourself or life.

Choose one from your list of Persephone situations, and make a story-plan. Start from the theme 'Someone is displaced from their normal life':

a) Ask, who? Who is displaced? Sketch your main character.

b) Ask, what? What is the situation – who or what has displaced him/her?

c) Ask, how? How does he/she feel – what is the difficult emotion?

d) How is the situation resolved, so that they feel better?

Write the story.

These are bittersweet stories, which always involve both a loss and a gain. The way to approach them is by really feeling the emotion. As Jung said, we connect with the archetypes through 'the bridge of the emotions'.

When you are writing about emotions, feel where they are in your body. Let your reader feel the emotions your protagonist is feeling by describing the physical sensations – a pulsing temple, a warm glow, a shiver down the spine…

Each individual will have dominant story themes and characters which run through all their life and writing. Androcles, Persephone and the Prodigal Son, are some of mine, and you will have your own.

At different moments, different stories may move centre stage, and these will energise your writing in the same way as dreams do, because they are relevant and have emotional charge for you right now.

To find your myth of the moment, try this exercise.

Myths of the moment

Make a list of the first six myths, fairy stories and traditional tales that come to your mind. Don't censor or select – just write whatever comes.

Try to summarise each one briefly, to check you have the basic structure.

Select the one you most fancy working with. If it happens to be one you can't remember in all its detail, refresh your memory by looking it up before you begin.

Take the theme – 'Someone is doing something' – and construct a new, contemporary story around it.

Persephone eats the fruit of knowledge, like Adam and Eve, and can never fully return to the innocence of childhood. Androcles confronts his fear and becomes a free man. The prodigal son leaves, grows and is reconciled.

These myths cover different areas of human experience; a master-myth such as the hero's journey covers them all. If you haven't read it, Joseph Campbell's wonderful book, *The Hero with a Thousand faces* explores this master-story in depth.

Master stories – the hero's journey

This is the basic structure.

i) <u>Departure</u>
Ordinary world   *In fiction, the set-up*
Call to adventure   *The spark – the hero has a problem/goal*
Refusal of the call   *Doubts/fears*
Meeting the mentor   *Help/support*
Crossing the threshold   *Engaging with the adventure – climax of this section*

ii) The road

Tests, allies, enemies *The hero tries and fails to solve his problem/reach his goal several times – in stories, often the 'magic 3' – tension builds as failure makes him more desperate to succeed*

Ordeal *Final effort*

Reward/treasure *Moment of triumph – climax of this section*

iii) Return

Refusal of the return/ rescue from within *Psychological adjustment of hero*

Crossing the threshold *Back into the ordinary world*

Bringing the treasure home *The hero and his ordinary world are changed – climax of the story*

The hero's journey is explored in countless other books on different themes including, of particular interest to writers, *The Writer's Journey* by Christopher Vogler, in which he analyses various blockbuster films to show the underlying hero myth, and considers the adventure of writing itself and the making of each individual story as a hero's journey.

The point is that this pattern could be applied to virtually every area of every life, because it's about movement and growth. Every time we do something new, we follow this pattern, and when we achieve our goal, our world is changed.

I often use this template in workshops to discuss the structure and dynamic of stories, which almost always start with a protagonist, present him with a challenge, make him strive to achieve his goal, crank up the tension through a series of setbacks, and finally see him succeed.

In case you haven't noticed, the hero's journey is also the basic pattern for the Senoi approach to creative dreaming, which is about setting out on the journey of the dream, confronting enemies, finding allies, and bringing home a reward.

Look out for it in television dramas, films and plays, novels, and in the stories of waking life. When you are looking, you will start to see it everywhere. You have probably already seen that it's the template for this book.

In *Writing the Breakout Novel*, Donald Maass suggests deliberately harnessing the power of the zeitgeist, focusing on the big themes of the moment and universal or cultural values as a way for authors to step things up from midlist to mega-bestselling.

One of the exercises he recommends is making three lists of your protagonist's motivations. The first list is of their physical and emotional needs. The second one is their secondary needs, such as support or avoidance. The third list is their higher motivations, for example a thirst for justice or a need for hope.

Normally, we write with the first list at the forefront of our mind, but Maass suggests experimenting with reversing the priority, rewriting a scene with the character driven by their highest motivations first. When I tried it, I found this really does feel different. It adds passion to the action, and speaks to the universal rather than just the individual reader.

Man lives consciously for himself, but is an unconscious instrument in the attainment of the historic, universal, aims of humanity.

Leo Tolstoy

When you create a daily practice of writing or remembering your dreams you gradually discover a consistent inner world with its own characteristic themes and images. You become attuned to its echoes in your waking life.

But as you fish for the secrets of your personal inner world, you soon get a sense that you're dipping into something deeper. You find things in your dreams or writing which seem to come from someone or somewhere else.

In dreams, you may start picking up threads from the dreams or waking life of those around you. You may encounter themes or figures which have a larger-than-life quality. You may find objects you have no personal experience of at all.

When you dream an unfamiliar name or word, such as 'Thaddeus', 'Sylvia' or 'iridium,' always look it up. Check whether it refers to something which exists in waking life.

As you begin to explore the wider hinterland of your dreams, this is where symbols dictionaries can come into play. They should never be used as a first resource, but once you have explored your personal relationship with a symbol, it can be interesting to look into its cultural and traditional meanings, to investigate any archetypal resonances.

Be careful, however, with dictionary definitions. They may augment the symbol for you, but on the other hand they may have no relevance at all. Follow your emotions and intuition when considering the historical and cultural possibilities of your personal dream symbols.

In writing, you may also feel yourself tapping into something bigger. The book I began writing about aliens on holiday was just before the curve. My new agent advised me to abandon it, as no adult reader would ever take aliens seriously, but a year later *The X-Files* hit TV screens all over the world, documentary makers investigated Roswell and other alleged alien cover-ups, and UFO sightings were being reported throughout the mainstream media, including the national news.

A book I started a few years later was about someone in a coma, but I didn't finish it because suddenly several high-profile books on coma came out. My Young Adult novel, *Drift*, was almost taken on by two publishers, but finally rejected on the grounds that they had both just signed up books about the same theme of sibling suicide.

It can feel as if publishers produce artificial duplications, trying to cash in on the success of, say, a book about wizards or vampires, but such themes will only take hold if they reflect something that's already happening in the collective psyche, and are in tune with current developments in our dreams, values and understanding of the world.

There's a whole subsection of autobiographical books at the moment which is sometimes called 'tragic lives'. They are based on the classic triumph-over-adversity model, but predicated upon the idea of bad parents and damaged children, which are part of what James Hillman calls 'psychology's fairy-tale'.

I'm not saying that bad parents don't exist and children's lives aren't damaged by them; I'm not questioning the credentials of these writers. But the reason these stories have such wide appeal is because they resonate with our cultural understanding of ourselves, which is based upon the popular understanding of psychology.

Psychology is changing and developing, with more acknowledgement of the influence of siblings, family dynamics, peer groups and social values in a child's development, instead of only putting parents in the frame. There is also more recognition of the spiritual dimension.

As these developments become more widely accepted and understood, the myth will change and so-called misery memoirs may lose some of their dominance in the best-seller lists.

As dreamers and writers, we can glimpse the archetypes behind our themes and characters. We can get a sense of the collective unconscious or zeitgeist which energises our dreams and stories. This awareness expands our self-concept beyond the waking 'I' and the dream 'I' to the mythic 'I'.

It is an experience of relationship in depth with other people everywhere, and through the millennia. It is spiritual fellowship as opposed to social interaction. It connects us on a deep level with readers we will never meet.

In dreams and stories, including the stories of our lives, we put faces on the faceless ones. Our personal mother carries all the aspects of the universal mother, and other 'mother figures' may carry particular aspects: Auntie Jean may be the good mother, and Mrs Bunce next door, the terrible devouring one. Our protagonist's relationship with his boss may carry the power of the archetypal father-son relationship. Sherlock Holmes, in our dream, may be the human face of the magician.

But human images are weak reflections of the archetypes and if we want to engage with their full power the only faces we can put on them are the faces of gods and angels.

2 Gods and Angels

If one works seriously with dreams for any length of time it is hard not to develop some degree of mystical awareness, for the dreams become more profound, more mythic, more 'religious', and expose one to experiences unmistakably suprapersonal and transcendant.

Anthony Stevens

Mythic and archetypal figures in history and literature have a larger-than-life quality, which speaks to us across centuries and cultures. For example, the characters in Shakespeare, whilst being fully realised as individuals, also carry qualities such as foolishness, jealousy, or ambition on the grand scale.

Kings and queens, princes and princesses, have always been archetypal figures; they are symbols in the common psyche as well as real people. The extraordinary outpouring of grief after Princess Diana's death was not only for Diana, the woman, but for the good, kind, beautiful princess archetype she embodied.

In the modern world, celebrities fulfil the same kind of function, and we see their stories played out in the media just as the stories of kings and queens were once played out on stage.

These are stories of towering ambition or God-given talent or exceptional beauty, let loose in the world and then often brought down, broken open so we can see how it works, and feel how it might work inside ourselves.

As we deepen our awareness of the universal qualities in ourselves and other people, and feel the power of the myth at work in the everyday world, our dreams and creative life take on an extra dimension, simply because of that awareness.

It first manifests in dreams as a mythic or larger-than-life quality around archetypal figures like 'the teacher', 'the old woman' and 'the king', but that soon opens the door to a quite different kind of dreaming experience, which Jung called 'numinous'.

Numinous dreams are more than larger-than-life. They are not of this world. They might include colours we have never experienced in waking life, and have no words for; numbers and shapes which seem to have mystical power; spirits and energies which wear the faces of gods and angels.

These are transforming dreams. They are spiritual experiences for the dreamer, which he or she will bring back into their waking life as a sense of wonder.

When this begins, the voice of the dream, rather than seeming like the highest wisdom within the self, can feel like the voice of God. It doesn't trouble itself with mundane matters, but pronounces on big issues such as life, aging and death.

I see blues, reds, oranges, but vibrant, vibrant pink. The squares have names, and my vibrant pink one is called Belief

The arrival of the faceless ones did not change the whole of my dream-life. Most of the time, my dreams were still like a TV soap, with a core cast of people I knew in waking life engaging in mundane activities. They were often, though by no means always, linked in obvious ways to my day-world.

The old man, the old woman, the radiant baby and other mythical figures visited maybe two or three times a week, bringing with them a change in the atmosphere of the dream. Then, they began to herald a different kind of dream altogether.

These dreams were strange, but not in the same way as my early dreams had been, where incongruous and impossible things happened in a random way. They had a whole different kind of landscape, which was as consistent as the landscape of my normal dreams. It felt as if, during my travels in the dream-world, I occasionally pushed on further, into a more exotic and less familiar place.

If my normal dreams were like a soap, these mythic dreams were like science fiction. I, the dreamer, was a hero on an epic quest, in a land of gods and angels. Baal came into my dreams, and 'Odin's horn'; Vishnu, Maat and Hathor. Not knowing anything about these gods, I looked them up. I understood them as symbols for the archetypal energies which powered the human psyche.

There was usually an old man or woman somewhere in the background, watering the garden or manning the reception desk or resting after a climb. Whatever the context, it would be vibrantly coloured, as if everything was lit from inside, and it would be unlike any scenery I had ever seen in real life – forests of huge flowers, crystal waters crammed with fish, smooth sweeping mountains and purple plains.

The buildings in these dreams were ancient, sacred places;

they were temples and churches, filled with treasures; they were lit by sunlight through bright coloured windows, or the soft glow of candlelight fading into darkness.

These sacred places had an air of mystery, and deep wisdom. I entered them with a sense of being given access to something I could not yet understand, as in this dream-within-a-dream: 'I was in a church or sacred building, and I stood transfixed by two round windows and two rectangular ones, each fantastically beautiful. I didn't know what the images in them meant, but I felt they were giving me direction. I woke up and started to write down the dream, feeling full of wonder'.

In another dream, I saw a lettered billboard outside a very ancient building. At first, I couldn't make out what the writing said, but then I saw it was, 'Child and Agnes'. I wondered, 'What does it mean?'

Sometimes, I had dreams which seemed to be just statements, with no narrative or images at all. I would wake up with words in my head, which gave me the same sense of being given something I could not yet understand. 'Dead people wait for golden dreams' – that was one of them.

'A word is a memory, but language is an instinct' – that was another. They could be short and pithy, or slightly longer, such as, 'Redemption comes through love, not fear. It's like a geranium – you cut the flowers as they die, and fresh ones keep on coming, all the way through the summer.'

Often, these word-dreams were about the meaning of life. 'The secret of the meaning of life is a rectangle, a circle, a square and a spiral' or 'The meaning of life is the exact spot in the middle of an L...'

The word-dreams sometimes extended to whole stories, so I would wake up with the words of a story but no sense of having been personally involved. The tone and content of these story-dreams was mystical or religious, as in this one: 'A woman felt her husband wouldn't want her, as she was old. She went to God and asked to be young again. She came back, with veils flowing around her, shapes and shades of herself. She did look younger. "You fool," they said. "You asked for youth and he has given you death."'

A large number of these sacred-place dreams, word-dreams and story-dreams featured shapes and numbers, which seemed to be imbued with meaning. The numbers 22 and 8, which I had noticed running through my whole dream-life like a thread, became even more prominent, and were often remarked upon by the voice of the dream.

I dreamt: 'I am afraid it's getting close to 7:42. Someone tells me, "Don't be afraid – it's 20 to ('twenty-two') 8 approximately – think of it like that. You've been through 20 to 8 before."'

The shapes were always circles, squares, rectangles, spirals and L-shapes. At various times, the dream told me that each of these were the meaning of life. The voice in these dreams only talked about philosophical things. It seemed louder and more important, even though I could not understand what it said.

Sometimes the voice of the dream was like a summoning call, so loud that it woke me up: 'I hear a clatter – a tape-box falling on the ground. It's loud, like real life cutting across my dream. The box has a symbol on it, a spiral or backwards swastika. Time is going backwards, in two-hour sections, instead of forwards, one hour at a time. And I hear a doorbell, whose ring is reversed. Soon now, I'll be able to answer it, and see who's there…'

If the voice of my dream had a name, it was God. The first time I dreamt the indescribable colour, it was God who told me to stay, enjoy and be amazed: 'I had climbed a high mountain, and near the top, I looked down and saw a lake far below, which was like aquamarine, but not aquamarine – a colour so beautiful, it took my breath away. I felt I shouldn't even look at it, but God said, "This is what you have come for, and you have earned it."'

After that, every time I dreamt about that colour, it felt like a gift especially for me, and I immersed myself in it. It came when I needed reassurance, as in a dream where I was running crazy-scared, and a woman beckoned me into her garden, which ran down to the sea: 'I plunged into the clear, deep water, so so aquamarine. The water sucked me straight out, with a whoosh, and I screamed with delight. I was not afraid. When it stopped, I swam back.'

I didn't know what these strange dreams meant, but I absolutely believed that they did mean something, and their meaning would be revealed to me. It was more than twenty years since my brush with Billy Graham had convinced me that religion was a sham and God did not exist. Now dreams were restoring me to my childhood faith, which was not a philosophical position but an instinct, not a doctrine but an experience.

God seemed to be present and to speak to me in my dreams, and so he/she became part of my waking reflections upon them. I had no doubt, as I wrote it down, about who the 'owner' was, in the dream about life that I called 'God's holiday cottage'.

'We're in a holiday cottage... While we've been here, we've worked to make the garden pretty for the next people, and we've got plenty of food in for them. It might be that they change it all, to make it how they want it, but at least we will have worked to make them feel welcome. We'll remember the work too, as something we really enjoyed. And the owner will be pleased.'

If I wasn't sure what was happening to me, my dream made it clear. 'I have a sheet of grey squares and as you look at them through an eye-glass, they change colour. I see blues, reds, oranges, but vibrant, vibrant pink. The squares have names, and my vibrant pink one is called Belief.'

Meanwhile, my day-life centred around the children, my writing, the beach and the pub, and there wasn't anyone I could talk to about what was happening in my dreams without them thinking I had lost the plot.

I wasn't on my own for long, however, because around that time, the New Age came to Cornwall. Shops sprang up where you could buy pictures and figurines of the gods and goddesses I was dreaming about; you could buy books about symbols, angels and sacred geometry; you could get information about mind-body-spirit practitioners of every kind who lived in the local area.

Suddenly, I was meeting people who experienced the world the way I did, as more than what we can understand rationally or through our senses. They seemed to be talking about the same experiences, but using a different language.

For example, what they called 'the akashic records' seemed to refer to something very similar to the universal layer of human experience and knowledge I knew as the collective unconscious. Some of what they called energies and spirits seemed to correspond to the archetypes.

The New Age attitude was open and experimental. You could try working with different deities and religious symbols, and develop your own practice from whatever worked for you. You could have a spiritual life without rigid rules and structures, and be part of a spiritual community without any doctrine or hierarchy. Women participated on an absolutely equal footing with men.

I enjoyed meditating and sharing my thoughts with other people, or tuning in on my own at home at an agreed time with others all over the world in, for example, meditating for peace, something which was suddenly possible because of the Internet.

But I didn't feel completely part of it because it seemed to me that the very openness which made the New Age movement so exciting could also make people gullible. The attitude of 'if I can feel it, it must be real, and anyone who can't is unenlightened' seemed as problematic to me as the scientific attitude of 'if it can't be scientifically proven, it isn't real, and anyone who thinks it is must be a fool'.

It didn't matter to me what anyone else thought was real – it was about my own personal journey. I took every opportunity to try new things – palm-reading, colour-healing, aura-photography, shamanic drumming, reflexology, reiki – treating everything in the same way as I approached my dreams, giving myself to it fully, but then assessing and deciding what I thought about it in the cool light of reason.

I was never convinced by claims and theories, but only by my personal experience. So I could never say, 'such-and-such is rubbish', but only, 'that didn't work for me'. And I couldn't say, 'this is right', but only, 'it works for me'.

A palm reader at the big New Age Fair in Newton Abbott told me I had a strong connection with France. I had done a French degree, and what she said reminded me that as a schoolgirl I had been convinced I must once have lived in France in another life, because it felt uncanny that I found learning French so easy and all other languages so hard.

I went to a past-life therapist. She took me straight back to a hot, dusty field in Normandy. I was lying in a ditch, hiding. I was rigid with fear. I recognised the ditch, although I didn't see the ants.

I explained to the therapist that I had always been able to speak French, but had an absolute dread of going to France. I had refused to go as an assistante in my third year at university, and the few times I had been since then, misery had fallen like rain on me as soon as we left the port, and not lifted again until we arrived home.

She suggested I do a ritual to clear any bad experience I might have had in France in a past life, and I did. It occurred to me that it didn't matter whether these ideas could be proved; what mattered was whether they could be effective for making life better. A healing in imagination was as much a healing as one achieved by a scientifically tested pill.

I had good experiences and bad ones; I met people whose intuitive gifts impressed me, others who seemed self-deluding, and others again who struck me as charlatans. But I was a casual visitor with all the healings and divinations – what really gripped me was the various ancient systems of knowledge such as tarot, numerology, astrology and Kabbalah, which had been hidden and were now made open.

It was through astrology that I finally understood the knifeman dreams. An astrologer reading my birth chart told me that one of the most important things in my life had happened six weeks before I was born. I asked my mother, 'Did anything happen six weeks before I was born?' and she told me, 'Yes, of course!'

Six weeks before I was born, Susan, then two and a half, fell into a coma. She was rushed to hospital, where they discovered she was diabetic. They stabilised her on insulin and sent her home, but my mother couldn't bring herself to do the injections, because Susan screamed so much.

So during the last six weeks of her pregnancy, my mother held Susan down across her belly, kicking and screaming, while my father injected her. As soon as she told me that, I thought of the knifeman on the other side of the door, the hiding and terror, and the screaming from somewhere outside.

I tried to study and learn about astrology, but it felt too complicated. Tarot was easier, because working with symbols was something I was used to. I noted there were 22 cards in the major arcana.

Numerology was intriguing, and it got me drawing and painting mandalas, to feel the mysterious energy of geometrical shapes and their numbers.

But the Kabbalah felt to me like the master-story – the one all the others could fit into. I painted my own tree of life, and put on it some of the other things I was learning. There were 22 paths, and the number 22 ran between Geburah and Tiphereth, which corresponded to Mars and the Sun. In astrology, Mars rules the sign of Aries, which is my sun sign.

The letter associated with the twenty-second path was called Lamed – in English, represented by the letter L. I did not try to construct a theory or analyse my findings; as with my dreams, I simply noted parallels and resonances, and enjoyed the sense of patterns emerging.

What I did, since I couldn't understand the complexity of the tree of life, was live beside the image I had painted. I felt it might reveal itself to me by a sort of psychic osmosis. I had done this with other, simpler symbols which had dropped into my dreams, and it was changing the way I looked at symbols in general.

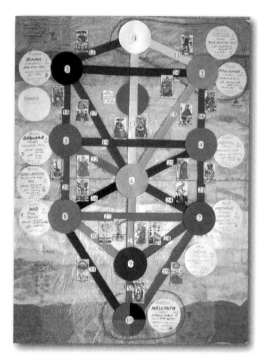

My tree of life picture

I had seen symbols as holding significance, reflecting aspects of 'real' life and being doorways to an understanding of spiritual things. Now I was beginning to see them as also being powerful objects in themselves, capable of creating change.

It seemed to me that everything started as pure energy – the nameless substance. This distilled down through the archetypes – the faceless ones, the spirits of, say, mothering, fathering, wisdom, jealousy, revenge.

Jung called the archetypes 'pieces of life itself'. They were real. You could sense them at work in the world, and in yourself, and therefore, you could name them. The spirit was the same, whatever name you gave it. Gentle mothering was the same human experience whether you called it the Virgin Mary or Kwan Yin.

From pure energy, to the archetypes or spirits, through their names, you came to symbols. The physical object was the densest precipitation of the energy. Icons and statues of religious figures were not just representations – they contained the actual energy of the archetype, which could be a transforming power.

I dreamt 'I met a symbols mechanic. He got into it by chance, by discovering that engines work better if there's a symbol on them, and now he cures mechanical failure with symbols, laying his little round discs on the affected parts. It shouldn't work but amazingly, it does.'

In my writing room, I had pictures and models of lions and owls, the animals I felt most drawn to. I had geometrical drawings and paintings. I had objects which related to the books I was working on – seashells or school books or photos. I used these pictures and objects not to represent, but to inspire.

One night, I dreamt about the name, Thoth. I woke feeling frightened, because, for some reason, I thought Thoth was a devil name. But when I looked him up, I found he was the ancient Egyptian god of scribes. The god of people like me. I bought a statuette of Thoth and put it on the corner of my desk.

I had been working for educational publishers for a couple of years, producing scores of books of every kind. I knew I was a disappointment to my agent, going down this byroad away from the High Street, where there were no prizes or foreign deals or big advances, and she had taken to communicating with me through her assistant.

I liked the anonymity of educational publishing, where the publisher and not the author was the brand. I liked the freedom it gave me to experiment with different kinds of fiction and non-fiction, plays and anthologies, across the whole primary age-range. I found writing short pieces easier to work around the demands of family life.

But, thinking about Thoth, aligning myself with the Thoth-energy, made me feel differently about my writing and myself as an author. The world of educational publishing felt too small or perhaps too shallow for me. It had been a solid apprenticeship in all the skills of writing, but the skills were not the writer.

I realised what I really wanted to do was write about dreams and symbols, so I put together a synopsis and some sample chapters for a book called 'Healing Symbols'. This got me an interview with the biggest publisher of mind-body-spirit books in the UK. The commissioning editor took my proposal to the next acquisitions meeting, but it was rejected on the grounds that I didn't have any academic qualifications in the field of symbols.

The editor invited me back for a second meeting, to see whether we could develop the idea in a slightly different way. She suggested that I try to rework my sample chapters from a more personal angle. 'I feel you are hiding in the material,' she said.

The idea made me feel anxious, even though I dreamt that when the book came out the publicity pictures, set in a remote cottage, made me look 'gentle and wise'. I tried to re-angle the proposal, and the editor did take it back to acquisitions, but it actually came as a relief when they turned it down again.

I had the writing skills but, although I didn't realise it at the time, I didn't yet have the dream skills to write the best book I was capable of writing on the subject. I asked Thoth, and all the other inspirational objects I had gathered around me, for an idea of something I might write instead.

Almost without noticing, I was moving from incubating dreams to answer my questions, to asking for answers directly, awake.

*The New Age terminology was 'channelling', which seemed to
me to correspond with Jung's idea of 'active imagination'. It was
quicker than waiting for a dream, but could be just as effective.*

*I was bringing the magic of dreaming into my waking life,
and it felt exhilarating and expansive. I dreamt, 'In a radiant
place, a little boy is swimming with the strawberry butterflies.
He charms them out of the water. They bring him treasures
from the deep.*

*'Sad people harpoon these lovely butterflies, stuff them and keep
them as trophies. I swim with the boy, and the butterflies come.
"I can charm them too!" I cry. "Everyone can charm them," he
says. "But most people don't try. They don't want to."'*

You have noticed that everything an Indian does is in
a circle, and that is because the Power of the World
always works in circles, and everything tries to be
round. The sky is round, and I have heard that the
earth is round like a ball, and so are all the stars. The
wind, in its greatest power, whirls. Birds make their
nests in circles, for theirs is the same religion as ours.
Even the seasons form a great circle in their changing,
and always come back again to where they were. The
life of a man is a circle from childhood to childhood,
and so it is in everything where power moves.

Black Elk

The circle is an archetype for wholeness and integration,
a universal pattern in nature and the human psyche which
is also a template for the stories of life and fiction.

Stories naturally make circles. The protagonist sets off,
achieves or learns something in the course of the action,

and returns changed.

Often the work of redrafting is about refining the beginning and ending to tie everything into a satisfying whole. The crafting of a story is a process of perfecting the circle.

Dorothea Brande says the unconscious is not only the source of our creativity, but also the home of form. This is why, when you have plot problems, new ways of fitting things together can naturally spring up in your mind as soon as you stop consciously trying to force them.

In this exercise, rather than moving towards the perfect form in your writing, you begin with it, harnessing the power of the circle archetype by deliberately placing it in your mind as a sort of map before you start.

The exercise is in two parts: making a mandala and writing the complete scene.

Making a mandala

'Mandala' comes from the Sanskrit word meaning 'circle'. It signifies a geometrical pattern based on a circle, and it's used in every spiritual tradition as a focus for contemplation, meditation, protection, healing or prayer.

In its most basic form, the mandala is a simple circle, and you can start by drawing circles. I recommend you do this freehand, although your first attempts may look like lumpy lozenges. Keep working at it until you can do one that looks reasonably round. The process of this will anyway help attune your mind to the archetype.

When you have drawn your circle, you can incorporate

other geometrical forms into it and around it. You could put a triangle inside it, crossed by another triangle to make a six-pointed star. You could put your circle inside a square, or squares inside your circle.

Choose any geometrical shapes you like, but try to achieve balance, so that the sides and segments of the circle are the same. Drawing geometric shapes also settles your mind into the beautiful reality of numbers.

Treat this like doodling, not trying to create art, but simply to play and allow your mind to idle. Keep building mandalas until you get one you really like.

Shading or colouring your mandala is a way of staying with the archetype for longer, and allowing it to work upon you. When you have finished, bring the energy of the circle with you into your writing. Bear it in mind as a template for your story, and see whether it gives you a greater sense of direction and clarity.

Some mandalas I've made in the
course of various writing projects

Writing the complete scene

Now, imagine you are watching a scene from a film. You will know how the scene ends before you start writing it, by doing three simple warm-ups. These warm-ups are short, timed pieces of writing, the idea being that you write whatever comes into your head, and keep your pen moving on the paper. They're not about starting the actual piece of writing, but about getting in the zone.

Start by taking a few slow breaths to calm your mind. Close or lower your eyes, and make the shift into your inner world.

a) The first warm-up is a snapshot moment from the middle of the scene. Freeze the film and look at the still.

In this snapshot moment, someone is pleased with something and someone else does not share their enthusiasm.

Notice their facial expressions and body language. Examine the background details – where are they, indoors or out? Notice the season, weather, time, place. What colours do you see? Is there anything incongruous?

When you have fully imagined it, take two minutes to write a description of what's happening in the still.

b) For the second warm-up, fast forward the film to the very last frame, and freeze it. Fully picture it. Take two minutes to describe what you see.

c) For the final warm-up, press rewind and go right back to the beginning. Freeze-frame the opening shot. Fully picture the image. Take two minutes to describe what you see.

Now, write some notes about the whole scene, allowing the details to develop as you ponder it. What is the relationship between the characters? Whose is the more interesting point of view?

Think about the structure of the scene. In what way do the beginning and ending frame the action, and how do they relate to each other? Can you use echoes at the end or foreshadowing at the beginning to connect them up? In this scene, you are looking for a transforming moment which is rounded off to make the point.

Finally, write the story. Take about 20-30 minutes. Notice how it feels to write the beginning when you think of it as part of a circle, related to the way the scene will end, and to write an ending which will refer in some way back to the beginning. You might not find the exact ending that clinches it until the redraft stage, but you are keeping the circular intention loosely in your mind.

Remember with all these exercises that you're writing first drafts, so the inquisitive child or experimenter should be in charge, not the critic. You aren't looking for something 'good' at this stage – you're in it for the adventure.

Images and the artistic process are the shamans and
familiar spirits who come to help people regain the
lost soul.

Shaun McNiff

'Where do ideas come from?' That's the question every
author must have been asked a billion times, and there
are any number of different answers we can come up
with. But however we explain our own creative process,
we will all have had moments along the way when we've
actually wondered ourselves, 'Where on earth did that
come from?'

Thomas Edison famously said, 'Genius is one per cent
inspiration, ninety-nine per cent perspiration.' So is writing.
Mostly, we draw on our experience and hard work to
develop an idea, but underneath it all there is always that
vital one per cent. Its source is mysterious, and mystery is
a definition of God. Creating something new from nothing
can be, like dreaming, a spiritual experience.

With writing, we don't have to understand, name or
even acknowledge the mystery, but we do have to learn to
open ourselves to it, to observe its rhythms and listen to
its voice. Many writers instinctively use objects and rituals
as part of their creative practice.

Some have particular pens and stationery for different
stages of the work – I know one writer who buys all new
pens before she sits down to start a new book. Others gather
ornaments or pictures around them, which relate in some
way to their characters, or items they have picked up from
the place where their story is set.

A lot of writers have lucky talismans or inspirational

objects which support them in all their writing, rather than just a particular project. I read once that Graham Greene used to take his childhood teddy bear on research trips all over the world. For myself, I have a painted beach-pebble paperweight one of my children made, which says 'Greatest work ever!' and I always use it to keep my current notes together.

Every time I finish a piece of work and send it off, I clean, tidy and polish my whole study, clearing my physical space as I clear my mental space for thinking about new ideas.

Every time I start a new writing project, I buy a new mug, which I will use for all the tea and coffee I drink while I'm working on it. If that sounds odd, I know at least one other writer who does exactly the same, as I found out by chance when I picked up the wrong mug at her house.

We don't have to name or acknowledge the energies which animate our creative lives, but in dreaming we may come face to face with them. In numinous dreams the nameless ones put on the masks of gods and angels, and the voice of inspiration can feel like the voice of God.

There is a danger that people who have these numinous experiences can feel they are being specially chosen by God to receive wisdom for the whole of mankind. I met a lot of people like that in the New Age movement. Their conviction made them charismatic; they were like gurus, who easily drew other people into their delusion.

I believed, because of dreams such as the strawberry butterflies, that anyone could have these experiences, but that most people simply didn't choose to, and that was absolutely understandable. It took patience, practice and devotion to the quest; it brought fear and confusion as well as joy and wonder.

If you come to dreaming and stay with it, you can have numinous experiences; if you practise any artistic process, you can be touched by inspiration. But these are enlightenments for yourself, not the world. It is your own personal compass, helping you to align with 'the lost soul'.

And it comes at a cost.

Enlightenment means literally the bringing of light, and the land of gods and angels is a luminous place. But bright light creates dark shadows.

3 Darkness and Light

If you undertake spiritual practice, you will be confronted by your dark side. This is an axiom... Seeking truth means experiencing pain and darkness, as well as the clear white light.

William Carl Eichman

Sooner or later, dreaming becomes a mystical experience, but when you walk in numinous landscapes with gods and angels, and when the magic spills over into your waking life, then you will encounter your Shadow. This can be traumatic because, suddenly, it's personal.

The Shadow is one of the major archetypes of the Self. It represents all the things you have identified as 'not me' during your formative years, when you were building your sense of who you are. It's the other side of the Persona archetype, which is your identity, or how you see yourself and expect other people to see you.

A classic depiction of the conflict between Persona and Shadow is *Dr Jekyll and Mr Hyde*, by Robert Louis Stevenson, which incidentally came to him in a dream. In the story, Dr Jekyll is a respectable pillar of the community, but he has a secret other side – at night, he is addicted to the pleasures of debauchery.

He invents a potion which can completely change his

physical appearance so that, as Mr Hyde, he is able to go out on the town and not worry about being recognised. Effectively, he turns himself into two people, one embodying his Persona, and the other his Shadow.

Whatever we don't identify as 'me', we project out. We may disown it so completely that we can't recognise it in ourselves at all. We can only see it in the mirror of the world.

One way we project undeveloped aspects of our Self is onto the people around us. A person who thinks of himself as hard-working and high-achieving may find other people lazy and unambitious. A person who thinks of herself as ugly may feel virtually everyone else is good-looking.

In a couple, the tasks of personality are often shared out. One partner may be good with money, so the other can enjoy financial security without having to develop good money sense themselves. One might be fun-loving and dizzy so the other can be sensible and steady, yet still enjoy a party lifestyle.

When a long relationship breaks up, you have to develop qualities in yourself that you didn't think you possessed when you were together, because your partner was carrying those for both of you.

On a collective level, cultures, countries and sub-sections of society also have a Persona and a Shadow. In our culture, for example, we identify female beauty with thinness, so our female icons tend to be underweight, but the shadow side is an epidemic of eating disorders and obesity.

In terms of mental health, Western culture is so identified with qualities of success and self-confidence that unhappiness and self-doubt are labelled as depression and low self-esteem, for which a large proportion of the population are on antidepressant drugs and therapy.

In his book, *Solitude: a return to the self*, the psychologist Anthony Storr points out that people we might consider 'poorly socialised' or even weird in modern society, because we identify strongly with sociable and extrovert behaviour, would have been considered perfectly normal a hundred years ago.

Individuals and cultures may disown their Shadow to such an extent that it becomes impossible for them to see it for what it is. We can't acknowledge the insanity of women deliberately starving themselves in a time of plenty, for example. We call that normal and demonise fat people. We can't accept that unhappiness is a natural part of human experience, a part of 'us'. We believe it is 'not us' – an aberration which must be curable.

On a personal level, refusing to acknowledge the Shadow and projecting it onto people around you makes for exaggerated emotional responses, and possibly conflicts. On a collective level, in families, it may mean one person becomes the black sheep, with all the family's unacknowledged problems projected onto them.

On a cultural level, the Shadow is often projected onto minority groups in manifestations of racism, misogyny and homophobia. At the national level, we may identify another country as 'evil' and consider it morally right, therefore, to go to war.

In religions which wholly identify with goodness and morality the repressed Shadow side may manifest in dark secrets such as the child-abuse scandal in the Catholic Church, or open extremism, terrorism, crusades and religious wars, because if we believe we are following the one true path of virtue then everybody else's path must be a path of sin.

But if you can look in the mirror of the world and recognise the other as potentials in the Self, these projections soften. Then, even if your opinion is unchanged, you are capable of making rational assessments of difficult people and situations, rather than acting out unconscious impulses.

Jung called the Shadow 'the seat of creativity'. Embracing the Shadow means opening yourself up to possibilities, letting go of fixed certainties about the Self and the world. It means engaging with complications and conflicts, which are necessary aspects of all creative work.

If you want to see your Shadow, think about people who provoke an exaggerated emotional response in you, either positive or negative. These might be people you know personally or public figures. The things you dislike or admire about them could be undeveloped potentials in yourself.

Notice what people say about you – both criticisms and compliments – anything you balk at could flag up qualities in you that you haven't fully recognised.

Consider anything which blocks your ego-desires, anything you normally fight against in life, as possibly carrying Shadow aspects. Physical symptoms which stop you doing what you want, for example.

See what happens if, instead of fighting, you side with whatever is bugging you. Ask it what it wants. Notice what it gets, in the effects it has upon you. This is always challenging – Shadow projections are only out there in the first place because you don't want to see them in yourself.

Experiment, but don't go at it like a sledgehammer. This isn't about instant insights; it's about attitude. It's about a way of being in the world, not demanding explanations, but open to possibilities, being willing to let go of what you think you understand without having to replace it with another understanding. It's about amplifying your experience to accommodate uncertainty and confusion.

Seeing the Shadow is subtle, like sensing archetypal resonances in personal symbols – it might be there to a greater or lesser extent, or it might not be there at all.

Judge by results. You'll know whether the Shadow is at work by what happens when you stop resisting the things and people in life that you don't like. The Shadow is an unwelcome visitor, but it comes to bring balance and wholeness.

For example, if you think of yourself as an efficient, capable worker but back problems mean you have to keep taking time off, the illness may be helping to bring balance. It may be forcing you to occupy more of your Self, more than just the part that is efficient and capable.

If you think of yourself as laid-back and easy-going, and therefore you resent it when someone you don't like keeps winding you up, maybe you need to learn to be a bit more assertive and stand your ground. It is possible to be too laid-back.

This works with a negative self-image too. Supposing you think of yourself as not very clever because you were a 'low achiever' at school – when you find something you're really good at, you might feel a great resistance to compliments and positive feedback because the idea of being good at something puts you out of your comfort zone by challenging your idea of yourself.

Engaging with your Shadow will show you things about

yourself you may not want to see, but that's the lesson of the Shadow – we are much more than what we want to be.

What I haven't done is put my stones in the wall of suffering. It's made of small and large pebbles. But now even the stones are being broken open – and it doesn't matter – they are symbols too. I see that now.

First, you learn things with your head, and think you understand. Then, the learning moves into your life, and you really do understand. I read, in a fascinating book by F David Peat called Blackfoot Physics, *that although we in the West think of the brain as the seat of learning, in indigenous cultures it is the belly.*

The idea of the Shadow was in my mind for a long time before I began to engage with it in my life. I knew what it was supposed to look like. I recognised it when I dreamt of a stranger, criminal or tramp – a nameless 'other' who, in my dreams anyway, often seemed to have tiny or deformed legs.

It was a dream that prompted me to look for the Shadow in my waking life, rather than just as images in dreams. 'I dreamt a passage from a book, the words and everything. It was good. I wondered who had given me these words. The narrator was a person's Shadow, being active (previously only glimpsed) in her life for the first time. She was put out, but her Shadow was delighted, and ready to flex himself…'

Another dream showed me where to start looking – in the people around me. This was a numinous dream, with that strange quality of landscape and light, and the sense of something important being given.

In it, I was part of a group visiting a golden monastery in the middle of a luminous mountain range. It was a very small monastery; it only housed nine monks.

The monks told us there were nine virtues, and they started to explain, but I wasn't really listening until they got to 'Travel'. Travel – a virtue? They said Travel had always been highly valued in the East, as a way of understanding the self and the world better.

The last virtue the monks told us was 'Simplicity', whose symbol was the elephant. 'Simplicity of the life alone,' they said, 'because alone, we don't know who we are; there's no certainty, and it's simple because of that. Only when people are with other people do they "know" anything, including who they are.'

I knew, in a theoretical way, that you could only see the Shadow in the mirror of the world, and now I began to look for it there, to try and understand how the people around me might be defining my ideas about myself, and carrying qualities I had, but couldn't see. I took note of the things I found most annoying in other people.

For example, there was one person in our social group who was always late for everything. Many dinners dried up and died in low ovens, while we all sat around waiting for her to arrive. We took to telling her that events were due to start half an hour before they were, but she would still be late.

I wasn't like that! I was always watching the clock, stressing to make sure I was on time. So I was shocked to discover, once I started looking out for it, that I was frequently late for things despite my good intentions – I just always had an excuse that made it feel like a one-off. The traffic was bad; one of the children was sick; I couldn't find my car keys...

When you glimpse your Shadow active in your life, you can accommodate it. I started to focus on what time I actually arrived, excuses notwithstanding, which meant soon I was allowing more time to get to things, and suffering less stress.

I knew the Shadow was made up of everything you didn't identify with, good as well as bad. People you idealised, as well as those you disliked, could carry Shadow insights for you.

I had read that siblings frequently represented the Shadow in dreams, and one of my idealised people was my sister, Susan. She was the Sensible One, the Clever One and also the Fearless One now, because instead of merely contemplating suicide, she had actually seen it through.

That was my idea of her but when I looked for it, I remembered she had had a quite different side which was the opposite of all that. Sometimes, she had been astonishingly foolish – such as the day she walked past large warning boards to wade across a muddy creek when the tide was coming in.

She must have been about eleven, and I about eight. Our parents weren't there, and I watched in horror as the water steadily rose up to her waist and then her chest, before she finally emerged onto the other side.

Or the day when we went into a field which had a bull in it, because Susan said it would be fine. The bull would ignore us, she said. But when we were half way across, it suddenly came barrelling towards us.

There was a stumpy oak tree in the field, and we shinned up it, just in time. We perched in the cradle of thick branches, barely out of reach of the bull, as it paced beneath us. Susan said we should throw sticks and acorns at it to make it go away, which turned out not to be a sensible idea at all.

I remembered how she had told us she was going to fail her exams, because she wasn't as clever as everyone thought. It wasn't only the drugs that made her fall behind with her work

– much of the time, she struggled to understand it.

And was it really brave to take your own life? Could that also be an act of cowardice? I still had those feelings sometimes, and when you're hanging over the edge of the abyss, it can take everything you've got just to keep holding on.

I could feel how it worked in me, pulling back these ideas about her being sensible, clever and brave, and reclaiming those qualities for myself. I was also sensible, as much as she was anyway. At school and university, I had been a high-achiever although I had never valued it, and I fought my suicidal thoughts, I did not give in.

Part of a woman's Shadow was the Animus, and part of a man's, the Anima. These were the masculine aspects of a woman's psyche, and the feminine aspects of a man's. The terms 'masculine' and 'feminine' referred more to energies – the former active and out in the world, the latter, receptive and still.

I'd been familiar with the concept of my Animus in my dreams for quite a long time, but now I noticed how it played out in my life. I had been entirely happy to stay at home and look after my children, and for my husband to be out in the world, forging his career.

He was confident and successful, and I loved that about him. I had been content to shine in his reflected glory, through the years when our children were little, like the moon to his sun.

But now I was working, I wished I had his confidence, so that I could develop my career as a mainstream author, and leave the comfortable anonymity of working for educational publishers behind. My knock-back with the symbols book seemed to confirm that it wasn't going to happen.

'I wished I had his confidence...'
I called this picture, 'The Wright Projection'

I went back to educational writing, including a retelling of Dr
Jekyll *and Mr Hyde, although I hadn't really noticed, when I*
chose that story, how relevant it was to the Shadow exploration
I was doing in my life.

But my dreams seemed to suggest that I actually could make
the career I wanted. In one, for example, I dreamt 'They were
filming Neighbours *in the London Underground. One of the*
characters had the tell-tale small, crippled legs. He had always
been in a wheelchair, but he suddenly stood up.

"'He's standing up!" I cried. "He can! He can!" He said
he had been in a wheelchair because that was the role he had
had to play. And I had always thought the actor was crippled
in real life…'

I woke up thinking, 'I know what that dream was about',
and when that happens, you can be fairly confident that you
do.

I decided to leave educational writing and try to establish myself in mainstream publishing again, only this time not with an adult book on symbols but in the area where I had a track record – children's writing. I pitched lots of stories and ideas, many of which got good feedback from my agent and publishers, but none were taken up.

The words they used most often were 'sweet' and 'charming', and the reason for their rejection was that my stories were too gentle for the modern market. I didn't want to write about villains or really bad experiences and I didn't see why I should have to.

It was the New Age. We believed in love and light. When I was in my teens, flower power had put a stop to the war in Vietnam and now the same innocent belief in goodness and the power of love seemed like a realistic way to engage with life.

While my career seemed stalled, life stepped in with a knotty problem. One of my children got into difficulties with bullying at school. My first impulse was to try and empathise. This was the era of the no-blame approach, where teachers acted as if the bully didn't intend the harm they caused.

The idea was that you simply had to make bullies realise that their victim was upset and they would want to stop; all you needed was to give them an 'out', a way of stopping without any loss of face.

I gave my child the often true, but also truly unhelpful, information that people who bullied had probably been bullied themselves; they had a higher risk of criminal behaviour and relationship problems in later life; they were often driven by jealousy of the intelligence/beauty/wealth they perceived in their victims. In other words, we should feel sorry for them.

Not blaming someone for deliberately hurting others, not

seeking just punishment, and disabling justified anger by encouraging premature empathy is as poor advice as you can give to a bullied child.

Most of the other received wisdom turned out to be patronising platitudes too. Children themselves know that telling a teacher doesn't always work, as ChildLine research around the time confirmed. It found that five to ten per cent of children will suffer prolonged bullying however well the school scores on all available measures. Children told ChildLine that telling could actually make matters worse.

Asking a bullied child to pretend he or she doesn't care/say something clever back/practise walking tall is also poorly thought-out advice, because by the time the bullying has come to light their self-confidence will already have taken a knock, and you're just setting them up for further humiliation.

I came to believe that we needed a much more robust approach. We would help our children more by acknowledging that sometimes shit happens, and no one can prevent it. It shouldn't, but it does. What's more, sometimes even people you think of as friends can be nasty and cruel.

When shit happens, you have a right to feel angry. You will also feel unhappy and confused, full of self-doubt and possibly self-dislike, but you will have to learn to handle those feelings. If you do, you aren't only surviving a bad experience of bullying in the present, you are also developing skills which will help you engage with setbacks in future life.

I researched the available books on how to handle anxiety, anger, helplessness, unhappiness and self-doubt. These were mainly American self-help books at that time, which were generally looked down upon in this country, but they contained all the seeds of cognitive behavioural therapy which has in recent years become the mainstream treatment in the UK for many kinds of psychological problems.

I learnt that if you change the way you perceive a situation, you can change the way you feel about it, and changing the way you think in general, changes your experience of life.

I found these ideas to be effective, practical and absolutely risk-free for children and families faced with bullying, so I wanted to make them available in a targeted way.

Thus it was that although I never planned it, I ended up re-entering mainstream publishing with two books about bullying – one for parents, Your Child: Bullying, and one for children, exploring the same ideas through stories, jokes and activities, Bullies, Bigmouths and So-called Friends. Both books have been through various new and foreign editions and have enjoyed consistently positive reviews and reader feedback.

It didn't escape my notice that my child's problem with bullying had absolutely forced me to engage with the reality of badness, even though I didn't want to. It had brought balance to my perception of other people and the way the world worked.

I saw how this new insight could give me the edge that had been missing in my writing. Before, I had been completely unable to create villains or any real sense of menace in my fiction because I only saw people as intrinsically good; I believed that if they behaved badly all you had to do was appeal to their better nature, let them see the hurt they caused and they would naturally want to stop.

Now I saw that there was a worse nature as well as a better one. Some people actually enjoyed having the power to make someone else suffer. All of us must have that capacity given the right circumstances – as John Lennon famously said, we are all Christ and we are all Hitler.

Having to confront bullying made life feel less safe to me, but also more real. Badness felt less bewildering and more like something that had to be engaged with.

It had also made me aware of an unacknowledged and unresolved problem of bullying in my family of origin – I myself had needed to learn the skills I was teaching my child, and that was a classic Shadow situation.

Could it be that my completely unconscious issues had contributed to this horrible problem for my child? The idea was deeply distressing. But it also made me more determined than ever to root out and confront my Shadow wherever I might find it.

Of all the 'bad' things I struggled with in life, the worst was my bouts of depression. I hated myself when I was depressed. I felt guilty because of the effect it had on my children. It undermined the idea I had of myself as a good mother, and someone who was capable and in control.

I decided to stop fighting it, but ask instead, 'What does it want? When does it come, and what is the effect?'

The effect of depression is inertia and isolation. You are incapable of doing anything, and you feel completely disconnected from other people, as if invisible shutters have gone down all around you. It's a frightening negative space if you fight it, but when I stopped fighting it I found it suddenly less frightening.

My depression became like a neutral, empty space when I surrendered to it. I gradually recognised it as part of my natural rhythm, slow time which restored calm when it felt as if life was spinning out of control, a balance for the other side of my temperament, which was characterised by huge energy and intense feelings of joy.

When I accepted depression as part of my normal life, part of myself, it became less dark, and that was exactly what was supposed to happen when you withdrew Shadow projections. Each episode passed more quickly, and without the devastating feelings of guilt and panic which had made it so much worse.

My lions helped. I had pictures of them in my study to inspire me with their fearlessness and strength, and now I was seeing their Shadow side too. Male lions were solitary for much of their life, a quality I was starting to acknowledge in myself, although I didn't want to. But you wouldn't criticise a lion for being solitary – it was simply part of his nature, so maybe I shouldn't beat myself up about it, if it was part of mine.

Jung said he stopped trying to cure his patients' neuroses because 'the illness is itself the cure' and I could easily see how that would work with psychological symptoms. But when I read that physical symptoms could be Shadow projections too, that felt more challenging. The concept of holistic medicine was in its infancy, and the body was generally treated in conventional medicine rather like a machine, quite separate from the emotional and spiritual being.

I was used to asking my dreams for information about physical symptoms, and the voice of these close-in dreams was usually clear and direct. For example, when I found a lump in my breast, the voice of my dream told me it was caused by grief at a recent miscarriage, and would pass.

I still got it checked by a consultant, of course, and he said I needed a biopsy, but when I told him my dream he agreed to postpone the procedure for a few weeks, and by that time the lump had gone.

But seeing physical symptoms as actual manifestations of the Shadow was different from asking for information about them, because it was about looking at them as symbols in waking life. They were themselves the information.

I experimented with thinking about symptoms in the same way as I might approach dream symbols. First, I looked for puns and wordplays – if I had a pain in my neck, was someone or something being a 'pain in the neck'? If I had a stomach upset, was there something I couldn't stomach? If I hurt my foot, did I feel like I was 'limping along' in any area of my life?

I considered the timing. What was happening in my life when the symptom started? What did it force me to do, or stop me from doing? What would happen if, instead of fighting it, I simply surrendered?

For example, the lump in my breast meant I couldn't become pregnant again straight after my miscarriage, although that was what I wanted to do. I had to wait until I was sure it wasn't cancer, and that delay gave my heart time to grieve and my body time to recover from the trauma and the anaesthetic. I had felt frustrated and fed up, but perhaps I should have felt grateful.

I found that if you took frustration, impatience and anxiety out of the equation, symptoms did seem to be less painful and pass more quickly. This idea was affirmed for me in a book I read around that time, Pain: the Gift Nobody Wants, *by Paul Brand and Philip Yancey.*

The book said that switching off pain was like disconnecting a fire alarm. Pain contained valuable information. It told you when something was wrong. If you listened and did its bidding, it could often show you the solution.

The authors talked about making pain less painful by accommodating it in your life, not panicking and resisting, or seeking to eliminate it altogether. They seemed to suggest that trying to eliminate physical pain was as unnatural as trying to eliminate unhappiness and emotional pain.

I read other books, at this time when we were beginning to see physical health in a more holistic way, by angry people with serious illnesses who resented the idea that they might in some way have caused their illness, and therefore be to blame for it. They rightly objected to the notion that you could cure yourself by simply adjusting your mindset.

But I felt they were missing the subtlety of this idea. It was simply an extra dimension, another avenue of understanding, an area you might explore. You might find nothing at all, or you might find a helpful sense of direction. It wasn't about rubbishing your current understanding, but rather adding new layers and possibilities to it.

It was like the dream journey. You might begin by thinking you could interpret everything in every dream in a psychological way, but when you discovered there was more in dreams than just bits of your personal history, that didn't mean you had to throw all interpretation out the window.

Knowing there were more possibilities simply gave you a wider context. It meant you could be more confident of recognising when a close-in dream had useful information about waking life, and more relaxed about living with uncertainty about the rest.

Understanding the Shadow meant seeing the unconscious as being not only a reflection or background to waking life, but also a major driving force behind it. It seemed that I was creating my reality, and that brought with it a dreadful burden of responsibility and guilt.

But although being prepared to know the hidden things about myself brought first a kind of hopelessness and despair, this was accompanied by a great sense of release. It takes a lot of energy to sustain an illusion, and when I stopped trying to make *everything fit my idea of who I was and how the world should be, it was like stepping off a treadmill.*

I was confused, but not afraid. I was used to holding uncertainty because of my journey in dreams, and I trusted that things would gradually become clearer. I dreamt that I needed this period of confusion, knowing that I was not what I seemed, in order to truly know what I was.

> **We select friends, and even husbands and wives, for symbolic reasons. And people we loathe correspond to neglected areas of our own personality.**
>
> **Tom Chetwynd**

You can use autobiographical writing to explore the Shadow side of your personality. Here's an exercise designed to help you see some of the unacknowledged aspects of yourself that you may be projecting onto other people.

Writing the Shadow

The exercise starts with some Shadow writing warm-ups.

Shadow warm-ups

a) List five personal heroes – these could be public figures such as politicians, artists and celebrities, personal acquaintances such as colleagues and family members, or fictional characters from books and TV. Write down the first ones which come into your head.

Next to each name, list three things you admire about them.

List five people you strongly dislike.

Next to each name, list three things you dislike about them.

b) List three physical ailments you have suffered from. These may be chronic and recurring, or one-off and acute.

Write stream-of-consciousness about each one for ninety seconds, going with whatever comes into your head, not censoring yourself.

The argument

Think of a big argument you've had with someone – it doesn't matter where or when or who. Go with the first example which comes into your head.

Take a few minutes to recall it strongly. Use all your senses to be back in that place. Feel where the emotions are in your body.

Give yourself fifteen minutes to write the scene, from your own point of view, as 'I'. Enjoy it. Don't hold back. Don't censor yourself, because no one else is going to read it.

When you've finished, take a deep breath and calm down!

Now, imagine you are the other person. Take a few minutes to fully imagine it. What can you see, hear, taste, smell, touch? What are your emotions, and where are you feeling them in your body?

Give yourself fifteen minutes to write the scene from

their point of view, using the first person, 'I' and 'me'.

Finally, imagine there's a third person who overhears the whole thing. It could be someone standing on the doorstep ringing the bell, but not managing to be heard above the row. It could be someone waiting at the bus stop outside the window, or trying to have a quiet snooze in the sun if the argument is happening out of doors. It could be a real person you know or a random stranger you've invented. Listen to the argument again. Really be there, as this observer, overhearing it.

Once again, give yourself fifteen minutes to write the scene, but this time from the point of view of the impartial observer.

Switching points of view is a good way of seeing things in the round, and opening up to other possibilities besides the narrow ego's-eye view of events.

When you are creating fiction, consider the Shadow side of your characters' personalities, which will be the opposite of how they see themselves and how they normally behave.

If your protagonist is generally confident and out-going, remember they are capable of feeling self-doubt and social anxiety. If they are caring and kind, they will also carry some potential for self-concern and cruelty.

By the same token, look at the Shadow side of your villains. A cad may surprise you, and himself, by falling head-over-heels in love; a thief may also wish to give back, like Robin Hood, or a healer, to kill, like the notorious doctors and nurses who have been exposed as serial killers.

Being aware of the Shadow side will help you to create well-rounded characters, and may be important to plot development. The most interesting characters are consistent enough for the reader to believe in them, but capable of acting 'out of character', without being unconvincing.

> ..if we were capable of losing some of that importance, two extraordinary things would happen to us. One, we would free our energy from trying to maintain the illusory idea of our own grandeur; and two, we would provide ourselves with enough energy to enter the second attention and catch a glimpse of the actual grandeur of the universe.
>
> Carlos Castaneda

When you see your Shadow in the mirror of the world, you understand that what looks like 'reality' is in fact life refracted through the distorting glass of your individual psyche.

The rational, objective story everyone shares, such as the fact that today is Tuesday in the UK, for example, or that apples grow on trees, can seem like everything, but it's only really a small corner of certainty in a sea of possibilities.

A person who sees life purely from the rational viewpoint is, as William Blake wrote, looking through 'narrow chinks in his cavern'. He said, 'If the doors of perception were cleansed, every thing would appear as it is, Infinite.'

Beyond the rational viewpoint, there is a personal

subjective layer which makes everybody's 'reality' different. People, illnesses, events all have the weight of symbols in the way that we experience them.

And it goes deeper than just the way we perceive things – we actually attract and repel people and events according to the mysterious needs of the psyche. The unconscious is not only a reflection or background to waking life; it creates and powers it.

The more you feel the power of the psyche, the more you become aware of the limitations of the intellect. We want and need to feel that we understand how life works in order to be effective and confident in the world, so we define things in binaries, 'good' and 'bad', 'me' and 'not me'.

Thinking we know who we are and what the world is means we can make decisions and judgements, set goals and steer a course through life. But it isn't real; it's an idea.

Meeting the Shadow shakes the belief that we can understand life in a rational way. It shows us that nothing is as it seems. But we have to stay centred in objective reality and the rational viewpoint or we couldn't function in the everyday world, so the trick is to live 'as if'.

We have to meet the world as if our ideas about it are real, but holding the knowledge that they are only ideas; to act as if we know, but tolerate the truth of not knowing.

It can take a while to ground yourself in this position, because when you first grasp the reality of the Shadow it can be an experience of devastating loss. You lose your concept of what you are – what Castaneda calls 'that importance' – and how the world works.

You lose your trust in your own judgement about what is 'good' and 'bad' in life, because the 'bad' things might be necessary for restoring balance and enabling you to grow, and the 'good' things might be creating stasis and holding you back.

You no longer know what to wish for, what to be angry about and resist, and what to embrace and be grateful for. You can't judge other people harshly, when they might be holding a mirror up to yourself.

But there are also gains. When you relinquish the idea that you can judge what is good and bad, you stop struggling against life. You still need goals and preferences in order to move forward, but you don't attach to them so strongly. If something isn't progressing the way you want it to, you can more easily 'let go and let God', to use a commonly heard slogan.

Your idea of yourself cracks open, taking in infinite new aspects and potentials, both negative and positive. You find that when you acknowledge the demons, they are not as dark as you believed.

As you lose certainty about yourself and the world, and where the line is between the two, you gain a sense of fellowship with other people. 'The more uncertain I have felt about myself,' Jung said, 'the more there has grown up in me a feeling of kinship with all things.'

You feel more tolerant, because accepting your own darkness means you don't project it so much onto others. You perceive that there are mysterious connections, joining everybody in a kind of dance.

When you first enter the House of Dreams, you discover the inner world of your unconscious mind. Opening up to the landscape beyond, you find the unconscious connections between you and the rest of humanity, the collective unconscious or zeitgeist, the archetypes.

In this dream landscape, you may walk with gods and angels, but you will also meet your Shadow, and then you will find those connections in waking life as well. You will lose the illusion of separateness.

When you lose illusions, you gain uncertainty, and that is truth. The energy you used to invest in trying to force life to fit your notions of how it should be is suddenly released. No longer anchored by fixed ideas, you are ready to fly into the dream-space and 'catch a glimpse of the actual grandeur of the universe'.

Part Four

Into the Dream-space

The final part looks at dreams as gateways to realms beyond all human experience, both individual and collective. This is dreams as mystical experience, and creative writing as a way of tapping the mystery.

1 Weightlessness

Before you study Zen, mountains are mountains and
waters are waters. When you catch a first glimpse into
the truth of Zen, mountains are no longer mountains
and waters are no longer waters. After enlightenment,
mountains are once again mountains and waters are
once again waters.

Zen saying

Looking at the world from the rational viewpoint is
like seeing in two dimensions. When you shift your
position slightly, there enters a play of light and shadows,
and you realise things are really not as they seem.

Things are not as they seem because what look like the
plain facts of your life are actually distorted by ideas and
emotions, which turn everything into symbols of the Self.
The first glimpse of this is alarming, but it's also exhilarating.
It magnifies your concept of yourself and brings the world
of things to life, because suddenly everything has resonance
and personal meaning.

When you see that the way you experience the world is
symbolic, then you can sense what it would be stripped
back, without any emotional or conceptual attachments,
but simply the manifest world you can see, touch, smell,
taste and hear through your physical senses.

The senses are the other way we understand reality, besides through the exercise of reason. But the exploration into dreams, which leads through the realm of light and shadow, deconstructing the rational viewpoint, will sooner or later pull the rug from under the material viewpoint too.

Regular dream-recall leads to increasing degrees of lucidity, where the dreamer may be present in the dream as an observer or commentator, or like a stage director deciding the course of the narrative.

Many dreamers report that their lucid dreams are more vivid and life-like than ordinary dreams. These dreams feel like waking life, because the evidence of the senses is the same. When the dream feels in every way the same as waking life, the senses are revealed as also being illusions of the mind.

For dreamers and writers, this feeling that the ordinary world is not as 'real' as it seems means that the world of the imagination feels even more 'real'. Rather than leaving the 'real' world and going off into flights of fancy, we move easily between realities, which are all products of the psyche.

I lie down on my bed and I suddenly realise, I am the bed. There is no division. I am everything in the room. Everybody. The world. This is the All and the Nothing. It's so obvious! I've known it for ages of course – but suddenly, I feel it too.

After the success of my bullying books I set myself a new career target – to develop a body of children's self-help books which would be practical but also entertaining and funny, so that readers might go from one to the next, not because they had big problems but because they enjoyed my writing. That was my own experience of reading self-help – if I liked the way an author wrote about one subject, I was interested to hear their take on others.

I wrote a total of eight children's self-help books, across a range of topics including stress, self-esteem, learning, happiness and creativity. Again, they were very well received by readers and reviewers, but in children's bookselling the emphasis was, as it still is, very much on fiction.

Non-fiction for children had nothing like the presence of adults' non-fiction on the High Street, and there was no children's self-help section in bookshops at all. Booksellers didn't know how to display this kind of book, and even where they were stocked they were hard to find.

As a career choice, being a children's self-help author turned out not to be a road to riches, but it did fit well with my explorations into the nuts and bolts of reality. The point about positive thinking, and later cognitive behavioural therapy, was that you could choose how you thought about life, and that how you thought about it changed not only your interpretation of what happened, but also the actual course of events.

So, for example, if you believed you could achieve something, you would not only feel more positive and optimistic about it, you would also be more willing to work towards it, and therefore more likely to succeed. If you didn't really believe it, on the other hand, even if you had all the necessary skills and opportunities, you would be more likely to fail.

The first part of the cognitive approach was to notice your automatic thoughts, to actually pay attention to the stream of self-talk which went on all the time in your head and of which you were normally quite unaware. You might be surprised to notice, for example, that your self-talk included a lot of self-criticism or apologising.

The second part was about questioning your automatic thoughts. Is this way of looking at the situation true? Am I really a thoughtless/lazy/arrogant person? Have I really done something wrong?

At this stage, you also ask, are these thoughts making me feel good? Are they helpful? Then finally, you consider other ways you might choose to think about yourself and your situation, which would be just as valid but more positive.

A simple switch in the mind could change your whole experience of life. Supposing you discovered your self-talk was generally pessimistic and catastrophic, and you asked, 'Is this true? Is it helpful?' You might decide it would be no less 'realistic' to make a mental habit of always expecting the best, and that might prove to be a much more happy and productive way of being.

I was confident that I could build a body of self-help books for children and I did, but when it became clear that it wasn't a financially viable career path, I set my sights on writing mainstream children's fiction.

Alongside pitching fiction ideas, I started working on my symbols book again, only now it wasn't just about symbols, but everything I knew about dreaming. When I'd written about twelve thousand words, I showed it to a friend who worked for a literary consultancy. She suggested that it would probably find an enthusiastic niche readership if I carried on the way I was doing it, but if I were to start again and make it into a workbook such as The Artist's Way by Julia Cameron, it could sell a whole lot more.

So I lifted all the practical ideas out of my work-in-progress,

*devised a lot of new ones, and then built up an outline around
them for a workbook, which I called, 'The Dreamer's Journey'.*

*Most of what was left over consisted of bits and pieces of
my own personal views and dream-journey, which didn't feel
relevant to my workbook, but I didn't want to just abandon it.*

*I felt ready to stop 'hiding in the material', and decided to
try using these discards as the start of an autobiography. I was
used to working on several ideas in parallel, so it felt natural
to write two books about dreaming at the same time. My
autobiography was called, 'Pink Jacket'.*

Pink Jacket

*But writing autobiography puts you right on the interface between
fact and fiction, objective reality and subjective experience. It
makes you even more aware of the way you create the story of
your life, by selecting down, choosing your angle, and interpreting
the way things happen. You can't avoid seeing how you turn*

the people around you into characters in your story.

It made me ask even more, who am I? If I created the world through patterns of unconscious projections, then the world was part of me, and 'I' did not exist as a discreet entity at all. If 'I' didn't exist, where did the thoughts come from which created my reality?

I read a book by Mark Epstein called Thoughts without a Thinker: Psychotherapy from a Buddhist Perspective in which he said meditation was not just about creating states of well-being, but also about destroying the belief in an inherently existent self. I didn't understand it, but it felt important. It made me want to know more about Buddhism.

The self-help books I had read often referred to Buddhist thought, comparing the continuous, unconscious self-talk to the 'monkey mind', and the process of noticing it to 'observing the mind' in meditation. Books on Buddhism seemed the obvious place to look if you wanted to think about the nature of reality and illusion.

As well as reading, I contemplated Zen koans such as 'What is the sound of one hand clapping?' and 'What is your original face before you were born?' Little questions and stories specifically designed to confound the normal rational approach, and push you into a new, non-logical way of thinking.

I already knew that what happened in the world was not, as it had seemed, unrelated to me, but linked in some way to the pattern of my thoughts. I also knew that my feelings were not an inevitable response caused by external events and other people, but rather something I could, to some extent, modify by changing the way I thought.

Studying Zen took me deeper into that place where everything was no more than a thought in the mind – people, ideas, emotions, desires – and every day, I practised 'just sitting' meditation, learning to observe and not attach to my thoughts.

Sitting cross-legged on a cushion, facing the blank wall of my study, I imagined my mind as an old ruined tower on the top of a high hill, open to the sky. Thoughts came, and I noticed them, like a watcher observing the coming and going of birds, in and around my tower. Sometimes they landed for a few moments, but then they flew away.

The great appeal of Zen, as I understood and experienced it, was that it felt expansive, calm and still. But it also felt passionless and impersonal to me. It felt like avoiding the human journey, even though I didn't doubt it as a way to explore and experience the authentic nature of reality.

I was a mother, wife, daughter, neighbour, friend, and I wanted to fully engage with my feelings, even when they brought me pain and confusion. I could see that desires and emotions were the source of suffering, but they were still also the source of much joy.

It made sense to treat desires and emotions as ideas in the mind, but if you could detach from them, compassion was the only way left to relate to other people. The further I went with my study of Zen, the more convinced I became, and the less inclined to continue.

The thing I found most challenging about studying Zen was the loss of the spiritual dimension. There was no external god-power, no religious observance. Nothing to pray to; nothing to pray for.

The energies and spirits I had felt moving in the world, the gods and angels, the numinosity, had no existence except through me. They were another illusion, within an illusion.

I accepted it absolutely, as a theory, but it felt counter-intuitive. I had always, from earliest childhood, had a sort of god-instinct, a sense of mystery outside myself, of some invisible power which I experienced with awe and wonder.

So I gradually stopped meditating and contemplating. I felt I had learnt life-changing lessons from the experience and, once you had learnt something, there was no need to keep repeating the exercise, because you yourself were changed.

Studying Zen had changed the way my mind was wired. It didn't only place a small still centre of competence and calm in the middle of my storms, it also introduced a ripple of instability which went on spreading long after I stopped my meditation practice.

I had read that Buddha described enlightenment as progressive disillusionment. When you stripped it down, withdrawing your emotions and perceptions, exposing the symbol-making processes of the mind, all that was left was the physical world in the now, and even that was apparently an illusion.

I hadn't managed to get to grips with the concept that things you could feel, smell, taste, touch and see could possibly be illusions of the mind. All the rest could be ideas, but solid matter was solid matter, and to believe otherwise seemed a step too far.

Then one night I dreamt I was having coffee with my neighbour, when I realised, 'This is a dream!' There was nothing unusual about that; I was often aware and present in my dreams as both the 'I' in the dream and the waking 'I'. The waking 'I' often gave a steer if the action of a dream wasn't going well.

But there wasn't any action in this dream. It was just me and my neighbour, drinking coffee. It went on and on, with nothing happening, and I was starting to get bored.

My neighbour had a white knitted throw over her settee, and

I ran my hand across it, feeling the rough texture of the wool. There was a cushion leaning against the arm and I slid my fingers across that too. It was silky and smooth.

I knew I was dreaming… but everything felt exactly the same as in waking life. I had never noticed this before, or never so intensely; I had never stopped to examine it, because I was always distracted by the narrative of my dreams.

I leaned forward to pick up my cup. The handle felt hard and smooth as I squeezed my fingers around it. I could feel the warmth and weight of the coffee inside, exactly the same as in waking life.

I lifted the cup, and felt the warm rim resting on my lip, and tasted the rich smoky taste of the coffee on my tongue. I put the cup down and picked up a custard cream biscuit. I felt the embossed surfaces between my fingers, breathed in the light vanilla aroma, examined the colours, tones and shades.

'This is me,' I thought, 'and this is a custard cream biscuit.'

I bit into it, feeling it crumble and melt in my mouth as I chewed, the soft mass of it slipping down my throat, the fine dust of crumbs on my lips.

I knew I was dreaming, but the evidence of my senses said, 'There is no difference between this and waking life.' Then I woke up.

I felt the bed sheets, nestled around me like a cocoon and, shifting slightly, smelt the warmth of my body. I saw the line of sunlight coming through the gap in the curtains, razor-straight against the window, ribboning across the crumpled covers.

I could feel the sheets and smell their sleepy smell and see the sunlight streaming in, but that didn't prove anything. They might be no more real than the rough woollen throw and the silky cushion and the coffee I had seen and felt and smelt in my dream, no more real and solid than the custard cream.

All I had done was drink coffee and eat a custard cream biscuit, and everything was changed. Where 'just sitting' had only taken me so far, my dream had placed me in the heart of the impossible truth of Zen. It had blown open the walls of the tower.

I suddenly felt I understood what the people at university who had taken LSD had meant when they said it blew their mind. Most of them seemed to dismiss it as a weird experience on the way to becoming a teacher or accountant, but there were a few who never managed to completely connect with the normal world again. I had avoided recreational drugs, because I was afraid I would be one of those.

Maybe hallucinogenic drugs simply fast-tracked a person to this place I had arrived at through my long explorations into dreams. When the trickster mind stopped believing in its own trickery, a massive fault-line opened under you and if you didn't cling on, then you could fall through the deceiving surface of things into an abyss of bewilderment, where nothing made sense.

The difference was the journey. I had not been catapulted by chemicals into realities beyond the ordinary world, from here to there so suddenly the shock must either shove you clear or overwhelm you. I had come to it gradually and deliberately, one step at a time, crossing the threshold of fear, walking the dream-world in wonder, learning its language and building up skills to survive there.

I had been through a psychological process of developing self-awareness, and even in dream traditions which used hallucinogens such as the one described by Carlos Castaneda in The Art of Dreaming this was a first and necessary grounding step. Castaneda called this process 'recapitulation', which sounded similar to Jung's concept of 'individuation'.

I had acquired a dangerous knowledge – that you could not trust the evidence of your senses. They were shape-shifters creating realities here and there, dreaming and awake.

I had stood with one foot in this world and one in the other as the waking 'I' in the dream, but now I had crossed completely, and I was not afraid. I didn't need to understand, only to experience, and it was an experience of incredible lightness and release.

Because here was the thing: if the physical world was an illusion, and we could move between other equally 'physical' worlds, then death was an illusion too. There was no point in yearning for it and no need to fear it.

I dreamt, 'I lie down on my bed and I suddenly realise, I am *the bed*. There is no division. I am everything in the room. Everybody. The world. This is the All and the Nothing. It's so obvious! I've known it for ages of course – but suddenly, I feel it too.

'I am writing something now about the invisible thing behind everything. If there's an animal, there's a Shadow animal also, insubstantial. This is my dream. Then I seem to wake up. I think, "I am awake now."

'There's an old woman here, sitting on the windowsill in front of me. I'm telling her about this writing. I'm saying about the other reality and she says it's like a place under this one, and we slip up and down, and I say that's a good way of putting it. But it isn't about words really. It's something you see. When you have seen it, you just know.

'Suddenly, something happens to me. I feel this vibration, a loud noise in my head, and my eyes are open, but seeing something else. The woman is a green glow – first I see her *aura, then she is fading into it, and then she is a shade of pure light, and I can really see it, and I'm really afraid, and I've got this pain from the vibration in my heart, neck and stomach. I can't breathe.*

'I think, "Don't be afraid! Go with it. Fear is the enemy. It's what makes this hard. Otherwise, it's easy, it's nature, it's how things really are. I can bear the pain."

'I think I am having a heart attack. Am I dying? Am I dead? In a sense, I am dead, because my sense of myself and my body is gone. If this is how dying is, no wonder people appear to be in pain, and afraid, but you can hold on and bear it, because of the amazement, the brilliance. Because it's nature, and you're seeing another sort of real.'

Once upon a time, I dreamt I was a butterfly. Suddenly I awoke. Now, I do not know whether I was then a man dreaming I was a butterfly, or whether I am now a butterfly dreaming that I am a man.

Chuang-Tzu

In workshops, we use images to play around with the idea of multiple realities through creative writing. You can try it with any vividly remembered dream.

Playing with realities

Start by drawing the most vivid scene from the dream on large piece of paper. Take your time. This exercise is not about creating art, but using the drawing process as a way of spending time with your dream in order to remember it more fully and re-experience it.

Put in as much detail as you can remember from the dream. Again, this is not in order to create a good composition, but to help you to remember and re-enter the dream.

Writing warm-ups

a) Write the full dream narrative, exactly as you remember it, in as much detail as you can recall.

b) Choose one object from your picture – it could be something solid such as a statue, or something less defined, such as the cloudy sky.

Ask your object, how do you feel in this dream scene? What do you want?

Write for ninety seconds from the point-of-view of the object, beginning 'I feel...'

Write for ninety seconds from the point of view of the object, beginning, 'I want...'

The dream dreaming me

a) Imagine that you are the image that you've chosen. The dream is your reality. Be there in the dream scene. Imagine you can sense and feel. What's happening around you?

Make the scene come to life – notice everything you can see and hear in your environment, everything you can smell, taste or touch. Notice your emotions. This is your world, before the dreamer comes.

This is the set-up. Take five minutes to describe it in writing.

b) Imagine the arrival of the dreamer into the scene. What is he/she wearing? What impression do you get of his/her emotional state? What does he/she want?

Tell the events of the dream from your perspective, as the image, right up to the dreamer's departure back to their own world. This is the action. Take five minutes to describe it in writing.

c) Imagine yourself back into the dream scene. How does it feel now that the dreamer has left? Bring the scene back round to the beginning again, noticing in how you, the image, are changed by your encounter with the dreamer.

Take about five minutes to describe it.

This exercise is about imagining the dream as having its own objective reality, a separate place which exists before and after our visit, and is not limited to what happens while we are there.

It's a return to the experience of dreaming as journeys into other worlds, before the practice of psychological interpretation reduced the dream to a product of personality and we lost the daimonic dimension.

Row, row, row your boat
Gently down the stream
Merrily, merrily, merrily, merrily
Life is but a dream

English nursery rhyme

Things are not the way they seem. Everything we think we know, through the exercise of our reason or the evidence of our senses, is an illusion, a creation of mind. We don't live in an explicable world. We are part of a creative process, where nothing is fixed, all is movement.

As you begin to observe your mind, through positive thinking or cognitive therapy, meditation or the practice of dreaming, you glimpse the truth of this impossible proposition.

The path of Zen requires you to engage with life as a young child does, or an animal, not armed with abstract concepts and preconceptions, but ready to accept whatever you find, without putting up rational objections.

In the Christian tradition, Jesus says you have to be as a child if you want to enter the Kingdom of Heaven – you have to give up your attachment to the rational explanations and assumptions of adult life.

In creative dreaming, you willingly enter unfamiliar territory without any attempt to define or interpret, but open to whatever that world is, as you did when you were a little child in this one.

When you let go of the rational viewpoint – how things must work, how things ought to be – you may begin to see how things actually are. Physicists say 'solid' matter is actually made of energy. Dreamers such as Carlos Castaneda describe 'seeing things differently', as different qualities of light.

Once, I was driving down the motorway when, suddenly, I saw streams of light above every car, some single, some multiple, depending upon how many people were inside; energy filaments streaming down into each living being, as if they had dived from the sky on lines of light.

These strange experiences seem to only happen once for me, but that's all it takes. Each revelation, such as the lucid senses dream and the lines-of-light, stays with you and changes how you see your ordinary world.

It's the same as when you're writing, you only need to give the detail once – 'He got into his red Ford Escort' – and then the image is in the reader's mind; after that, the reader knows and you can just call it a car.

Through loosening your hold on the rational and material viewpoint, you enter the realm of pure creativity. At first, it may feel alarming, because there's nothing to hold onto. But nothing to hold onto also means nothing to hold you down.

Life is a dream. 'Row your boat, gently, down the stream', as the nursery rhyme goes. 'Gently...' don't resist. 'Merrily, merrily...' enjoy the journey. If 'life is but a dream', it could take you anywhere. It could take you through the veil of matter, and on to the end of time.

2 The End of Time

What dreaming does is give us the fluidity to enter into other worlds by destroying our sense of knowing this world.

Carlos Castaneda

If you write your dreams down over a period of time and then read back through them, you will probably find that some of them are predictive. They may not predict momentous events, but particular details and developments in your day-to-day life.

For example, when I was looking for a new house several years ago, I was focusing on estate-style bungalows within a ten-mile radius of where I was living. As chance would have it, my daughter and I were going to see a play in a village on the moor, some twenty-five miles away, and I noticed on a property website that there was a little miner's cottage for sale up there.

It was the wrong sort of house in the wrong area but, being curious, we set up a viewing. As soon as I walked in, I fell in love with it and made an offer. Looking through my dream diaries recently, I discovered I had had a dream a few months before that viewing in which I bought a little terraced cottage on the moor. The cottage in my dream, like the one I bought, was the middle one in a terrace of five.

In one workshop series, someone dreamt that her manager, who was on holiday at the time, came back early, looking pale and tired. A few days later, that's exactly what happened; her manager had to cut her holiday short because her daughter had been rushed to hospital, and she returned to work early looking pale and tired.

You can't tell at the time of dreaming, of course, that these seemingly inconsequential dreams are predictive, and you may not even remember them if you don't keep a dream diary.

People who don't have regular recall may remember a single vivid dream which turns out later to have been predictive, especially concerning the death of someone close. This seems to be a fairly common phenomenon.

I myself dreamt of my sister's death, and later my father's, a few days before they occurred, and I've heard lots of similar stories from friends and acquaintances. Only last weekend, someone told me about a particularly vivid dream he had had about his grandmother.

He was living in London at the time, far away from his Mediterranean homeland, and the dream was set on the hillside where he grew up. He was alone with his grandmother, and she seemed luminous, as if she was radiating light. All her wrinkles were luminous, he said.

She told him, 'Tell your mother I'm all right. It's much better here.' The following year, when he went home, he discovered that his grandmother had died, although nobody had told him.

There are also many famous predictive dreams, such as Abraham Lincoln's dream about his own assassination three days before the event. He dreamt that he heard sounds of grieving in the house, and went to find out what had happened. He eventually came upon a body lying in state, with soldiers standing guard around it. 'Who is dead in the White House?' he asked. 'The President,' one of the soldiers told him. 'He was killed by an assassin.'

Like dreams, works of fiction can also be predictive, because imagination can range not only through the close-in stories of the personal unconscious to the collective unconscious or zeitgeist, but even further than that, into the mystery beyond human understanding, which includes things that haven't happened yet.

In *Gulliver's Travels*, Jonathan Swift writes about some astronomers who have discovered two tiny moons orbiting the planet Mars. Real astronomers weren't able to see these moons until 142 years later.

George Orwell, in *1984*, foresees an age when surveillance cameras are on every street corner and screens in every home; when people are persuaded to give money to the government outside of their taxes, in lotteries, and police patrol in helicopters. The book was first published in 1949.

Edgar Allan Poe's novel, *The Narrative of Arthur Gordon Pym of Nantucket*, tells the story of a group of sailors who survive after a storm hits their ship. Having no food, they cannibalise the cabin boy, whose name is Richard Parker.

Several decades after Poe wrote the book, a British naval ship capsized in similar circumstances. Among the initial survivors was a cabin boy named Richard Parker, who was the first one to be killed and cannibalized.

Everyone has heard of famous predictive dreams and novels, and many people know someone personally who has shared such a dream, but we mostly dismiss such things as curiosities. They can't be real because prediction isn't possible.

Prediction is impossible because time is a line on which events build from past to present in a step-by-step fashion, and the future has nothing written on it except hopes, fears and ideas. No one can read words which don't exist yet.

It's easy to pass single predictions off as lucky flukes and guesses, but the practice of dreaming can reveal a thin but continuous thread of predictive dreams. Then theories about how things ought to work seem less reliable, and we may prefer to trust our own experience.

Dreamers and psychics know that time can't be the way we normally conceive it because, if it is a line, you can go forwards as well as backwards on it. But everyone who examines their normal day-life experience of time will discover something else – it is elastic.

It's a truism to say time moves faster as you get older, or when you're enjoying yourself, but we dismiss this as simply the way it seems to the individual. Yet there's evidently science and maths to back up the idea of the elasticity of time. I saw a mathematician on TV last night explaining that if a train was rushing through a station, people's watches would go faster on the station than on the train.

I can't pretend to understand the way scientists and mathematicians work out the nature of time and space because that's not my method. There is science that shows matter is not in fact solid, as it seems, but everything consists of energy. There are scientific enquiries going on right now into whether particles can move faster than the speed of light, which presumably would mean the future has already happened.

Scientists can explain in theories and equations why matter, time and space are illusions, but dreamers and creative people can experience it for themselves. The artist, Vincent van Gogh, said that our normal concept of time might one day look as primitive as the ancient belief that the world was flat.

Letting go of the idea of time as a line which travels in one direction has an interesting knock-on effect in terms of identity and the human journey. We see our nought-to-three-score-years-and-ten measured out in equal steps, of seconds, minutes, hours, weeks, months and years. We see ourselves as being shaped by events which have happened along the way. That's the psychological model.

But if at least part of the future is already in place, then we don't develop in a cause-and-effect way. There is a new influence in the mix – not just nature and nurture, but also destiny; the pull of the future, as well as the push of the past. And there is also a new question – not only 'What has made me the way I am?' but also 'What was I born to be?'

It's only in recent times that we've abandoned the idea of personal destiny. It's a challenging idea because at first glance it seems to mean that a person is not in control of his or her own future, in which case, what happens to personal responsibility, and what's the point of anything?

But if we let go of our common concept of time, there

are any number of other possibilities as to how it might work. Maybe some future events are laid down, and we join the dots according to our own choice of route. Maybe predictions are potentials, events which might happen in the way foretold; or maybe they're versions of experience the way memories are story versions of things which have happened in the past.

Or perhaps time isn't a line at all, and there might be any number of alternative futures, any of which we might glimpse in predictive dreams and fiction. Time might be a series of parallel lines, or a circle, or concentric circles, or any other kind of shape we can conceive.

The point about dreaming and creativity is that it is expansive. It doesn't replace one certainty, or illusion, with another. It dislodges all certainties and opens you up to a world of possibilities.

'What will happen, has happened…'

There are some friends you see all the time and never feel truly close to. There are others you hardly ever see, perhaps because they live far away, and yet you feel a very deep connection which endures.

I saw Anne several times a week during the time I lived in Shetland, but when I moved to Cornwall, I still felt close to her. We spoke on the phone a couple of times a year and sent each other occasional letters; that was all it took to keep our friendship alive.

When we were in our late forties, her grown-up daughter moved to Devon, and Anne came down to visit. It was wonderful to take her to all my favourite haunts, as she had done with me when we first arrived in Shetland so many years before.

But after her visit, Anne was taken ill. She was diagnosed with ovarian cancer, and underwent major surgery. As soon as I heard the news, I remembered the dream I had had more than twenty years previously, in which she had told me, 'In a minute, a big bee will land on my chin. It will sting me, and then I'll die.'

Feeling panicked again, I remembered the words she had used in the dream to calm my panic – 'What will happen, has happened.'

I felt a deep sense of foreboding. In that horrible helplessness, all I wanted to do was pray, but I had never gone back to prayer since my explorations into Zen had shown me that gods and angels were simply aspects of mind, like everything else. It would have felt silly, like praying to yourself. Or rather, as the self did not exist, like praying to nothing.

But now my need to pray was so strong, it pushed me into a new position. Just as I lived my daily life 'as if' it was real, because you had to do that in order to be in the world, so I decided to pray 'as if' the gods and angels were real, even though I knew they were only symbols in the mind.

At first, I tried to imagine it as I had before, with divine energies distilled down through the names of gods, goddesses and angels into their densest form of icons and images. I gathered objects, created an altar and used rituals, in the way I had previously done myself, and most religious organisations do.

It didn't feel right. It felt too small, too fragmented, too local somehow, in the face of the vastness of mind. So I left all the old ways behind and came to prayer as I had to meditation, in total simplicity, just sitting. When I started, I asked that Anne shouldn't suffer, and that she should not be afraid, and when I finished, I gave thanks.

For the first time, I used the name, God. Before, I might have said Great Spirit, or Life, and I would have meant that teeming mass of spirits and energies, gods and angels, at work in the world. But it didn't matter what you called it, whatever it was, that vastness where everything was created and everything dissolved. It didn't exist, or maybe it was all that existed.

The name of God, which was all and yet nothing, felt like a sheltering power. But unlike the gods and angels, it felt impersonal. Its comfort was the comfort of being in a wild lonely place and knowing your own insignificance.

I prayed for Anne every night and thought about her every day. She would text me her blood-test results before and after her chemotherapy. In the summer, when her chemo finished, I went up to Shetland to see her.

She had lost some of her hair, but she'd kept the soft roundness of her face, her pink cheeks and tip-tilted nose. I always used to think, when she was young, she looked like Marilyn Monroe might have done, without the make-up and bottle-blonde hair. She had the same smile, the same warmth and the same lovely girlishness.

Seeing her still looking bonnie and well, I could almost believe she was going to recover. But when she looked me in the eye, I saw she knew that she was dying. We talked about the years my husband and I lived in Shetland, the places we went together, and the new experiences we shared as we all embarked on the adventure of grown-up life.

We talked about what had happened in our lives in the years since then, but we didn't talk about the future, and when

I left, I didn't know whether I would ever see her again.

I had stopped writing the workbook, 'The Dreamer's Journey', to put all my energy into the autobiographical 'Pink Jacket.' I had written about my childhood and adolescence but the whole point about the book was that it was supposed to be about dreams, and as dreams had hardly featured in my early life, I wasn't particularly enjoying the writing.

I hoped maybe my interest would be rekindled now that I'd finally come to the Shetland period, when the psychiatrist had pulled the coloured silks out of the hat, and this glorious lifetime of dreaming had begun.

Starting with research, rereading all the dream diaries I had written in Shetland, I discovered a very peculiar thing. I knew I would find information in those dreams about such things as the progress of my first pregnancy, because I had asked for it, and remembered it being given.

But many of the dreams I had dismissed as weird and impossible to understand, exactly described events which were later to happen. These events were not in my body, like my pregnancy, but external to me, and there were so many of them it was impossible to pass them off as random coincidence.

Our first child was conceived in mid-November, 1979, and you will remember that the pregnancy ended prematurely when my waters broke after I slipped and fell on a slippery slope, and I was rushed to hospital and given injections to prevent me going into labour.

On 20th September, two months before our baby was even conceived, I dreamt, 'I was pregnant and on the way to hospital. There had been a flood, and we had to pick our way along embankments and ridges – I was frightened of falling. But I got to the hospital OK, and lay in bed.

'I had injections in my hips. Nothing happened. In a bed at the end of the ward, a woman was giving birth. Why wasn't I? All day, I waited for contractions, but nothing happened. They gave me another injection the next day...'

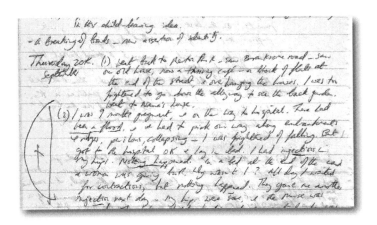

My diary entry for 20th September, 1979 – I underlined the main points years later, when I realised it had been predictive

When I had this dream, I not only hadn't conceived yet – we hadn't even started trying for a baby; we were still just talking about it. My notes on interpretation show that I thought it was to do with a new sense of independence I was experiencing, symbolised by the baby, but I couldn't make anything at all of the injections and so on.

On 13th November, again before the baby was even conceived, I dreamt, 'In the hospital, I had given birth to a tiny baby – so tiny it was kept in a glass tube container and fed through a tube, a constant flow of white. I thought the hospital had induced me too early. I wanted to feed the baby...'

I had never been in a maternity ward, let alone a special

baby unit, and I didn't know anything about the care of premature babies, so the image of the glass container and the feeding tube meant nothing to me. But when our baby was born she was placed in an incubator and fed through a tube, and when I reread this dream twenty years later, I knew exactly what it was about.

At the end of February, more than four months before the event, I dreamt about falling on my bottom on a slippery slope. The weather was different, and we were playing rounders with our friendship group rather than camping, but the people were the same and the place I had pictured in the dream was the same place I was to fall, near the beach below our friend's house on Burra Isle.

On the sixth of May, I dreamt the baby's gender and appearance. In this dream, my friend Frances came for coffee, and she asked me, 'What will your baby be like?' I said, 'She will be very tiny – dark haired – and her skin will be too red at first...'

A week before she was born, I dreamt, 'The baby popped out, so quickly, we were not prepared. Ian went to buy babygros etc...' It was exactly what happened. While the baby and I were recovering in Aberdeen hospital, my husband had to brave the alien territory of Mothercare to buy some baby clothes because, believing we still had six weeks before we would need them, we hadn't got around to buying any yet.

Finding so many precisely predictive dreams in these early diaries felt weird and disorientating. I knew that I'd had predictive dreams in the past, but those had had a particular quality. They had actually felt portentous. They were about the deaths of my sister and later my father, and I had woken from them with a strong sense of foreboding.

I had told my husband about the first one, and my homeopath about the second, and when the deaths had occurred, I had explained the dreams to myself by imagining I must have picked up some kind of telepathic message.

After all, my sister must have been thinking very strongly about what she was about to do during the three days before her death. She had planned it cunningly, so that no one would find her in time, as they had on her previous attempts.

My father probably wouldn't have known consciously that he was going to die, but it made sense to me that a person must know at a deep level when their body is approaching the final crisis. Maybe telepathy worked on that level too, from one unconscious mind to another.

The dreams I found when I reread my Shetland diaries predicted the details of events that hadn't happened, but they felt exactly the same as any other dream at the time of dreaming, and I would never have become aware of their predictive nature if I hadn't recorded them in full and then read back through my diaries years later.

How did it work? Which came first – the dream, or the day events? Could it all start in the dream? Was the dream there from the beginning, and the day-world simply a version of it, acted out? Among other things, that might explain the phenomenon of déjà vu.

How was it possible for a person to know, even in their deep unconscious mind, details of external events which were yet to happen, events that nobody else could have known about either? How was it possible to hear these echoes from the future?

I looked at the timeline I had written for my autobiography, where the events of my past were mapped out, one following on from another in a cause-and-effect way, building into a coherent narrative of what had made me the person I was, right up to the present moment, but not beyond.

What if the future was already in place? If what was going to happen had already happened, then it wasn't only where you had been that made you the person you were. It was also where you were heading.

Framed in this way, things like depression and thoughts of suicide, which in psychology's terms looked like illness and disorder, might actually have been part of my soul's purpose, setting me on this path of dreams.

I remembered the astrologer who had read my natal chart telling me I could be a writer or journalist, and that I had a big book in me which hadn't yet been written. If this was my big book – and I had been working on it in some form or another throughout my whole writing career – then my path of dreams could have been bringing me to that part of my destiny.

The idea of destiny was not difficult for me to embrace. Four times in my life, I had held my newborn child in my arms, and felt acutely aware of his or her unique spirit and personality, before any life experience at all had happened to shape them. They came out of the mystery, complete with whatever dream they were dreaming.

If I looked back at my own early childhood, all the big themes were there from the beginning. The idea of God was in me, although it was not in anyone else in my family, or in our family culture. The fascination with death was there as well, and the instinct to write.

Those objects were like a beacon, and my life had moved unfailingly towards them, through the medium of dreaming. The triumphs and the tragedies had all kept me true to the path.

But where did that leave the question of free will? It seemed to me that the natal chart was your soul's blueprint, like the genetic blueprint of your physical body. It showed your predilections, your strengths and vulnerabilities. It showed the likely themes and character of your life.

But you could make lifestyle choices which would make you more likely to realise either the negative or the positive potentials in your soul's progress exactly the same way you could in your body's.

If you had a genetic disposition to heart disease, for example, the choices you made about diet, exercise and smoking could hasten or prevent problems with your heart. You were in control of your own destiny, but within the parameters you were born with.

The astrologer had said I would only write my big book if I could overcome 'the considerable difficulties' in my chart. There was destiny, but you had to rise to meet it.

Astrology helped me understand how each moment in a person's life could contain both past and future, but it didn't explain how anyone could have knowledge of incidents which had not yet happened. It didn't necessarily shake the concept of time as a line.

Thinking about time in this way reminded me of my brief brush with the idea of past-life regression, years before, which took me back to that dusty ditch in war-torn France. According to past-life therapists, the line from future to past stretched back beyond your birth in this life, back and back through multiple other births and deaths.

This still seemed like the only logical explanation for my ability to learn French so easily, when I had no aptitude for any other languages, but meeting other people who had consulted past-life therapists had been enough to make me sceptical. An unlikely proportion seemed to believe they had been royalty or other significant people, and they only seemed to have found past lives in well-documented periods and places.

So I wasn't completely convinced by the idea of past lives. I thought past-life regression was more an exercise in imagination than a flashback to an actual former life, and my scepticism had been confirmed by a second session with a past-life therapist.

This time, I was a Jewish woman living in Austria during the war; I fled to Paris, where I was later killed. It felt like proof positive that past lives were imaginary because you couldn't have two lives which overlapped; you couldn't be two people at once. But now I thought, if you could travel backwards and forwards in time, why not laterally too? What if lives ran concurrently, as the dream and the waking life do?

What if life was not fixed to a beginning, middle and end, but on a loop, round and round, or concentric circles, with the same individual consciousness in the middle, living different lives? I had no answers, but I was exhilarated to have these questions, brand new questions I had never imagined in my life before.

If I had a big book in me – and I don't mean a big book in the sense of a ground-breaking bestseller, but a big book for me – the biggest book I was capable of writing – then I didn't feel it was 'Pink Jacket', at least not in its current form. It wasn't focused enough on dreams and it flew in the face of what dreaming was teaching me.

Autobiography made a life into a coherent story, which developed in a logical way. Everything was laid down along a timeline, one thing leading to another. Even if you played with time, by using flashbacks and flash-forwards, you were still as fixed on that line as a train on a track.

It was actually a relief to stop writing 'Pink Jacket' and go back to the drawing board. I wasn't fired by my life history in the way I was fired by my journey in dreams, so writing autobiography had felt disappointing, and anyway it still felt uncomfortable.

My doubts about whether it was acceptable to publish a story in which real living people were partially represented as characters, and call it a factual account, had never really gone away.

I had no idea how I was going to take my dream book forward, but if everything was already written in the stars when you were born, maybe I didn't need to worry about it. Its form was already out there; it would reveal itself to me.

> **Your profession is not what brings home your pay-cheque. Your profession is what you were put on earth to do. With such passion and such intensity that it becomes spiritual in calling.**
>
> Vincent van Gogh

If you're interested in thinking more about the idea of personal destiny, I can recommend a fascinating book by James Hillman called *The Soul's Code: In Search of Character and Calling.*

In it, Hillman describes what he calls 'the acorn theory', according to which we are each born with the seed of what we might become, the way the acorn holds the promise of the tree.

Instead of seeing ourselves as the result of early experiences, influences and traumas which, as Hillman says, make victims of us all, the acorn approach sees us as being born to a calling.

Everything that happens contributes to our calling, and we can speed or slow our movement towards it, depending on how strongly we are able to feel it and cleave to it. The task is to find out what is in our heart, what we most desire to do, be and have, and flow with the drive that is in us.

You may have been born to create beautiful structures, in painting or mathematics or creative writing; to nurture a family; to lead an organisation, an army or country; to entertain other people, or to live a life of quiet contemplation.

Some people are born with a great hunger to travel and see the world, to climb mountains, study other cultures, learn about nature. I think I was born with that hunger for travel and adventure, but into the inner world rather than the outer.

You may not be consciously aware of your soul's purpose. You may have gone through life never really knowing what you want or who you are. The clue is often in your first childhood dreams and ambitions.

As you grow up, the world makes its own demands and seeks to impose its own values. Then, even if you felt a sense of purpose and destiny as a child, you may forget it along the way. If you are lucky, you may find it again.

That's what happened to me, when I decided to become a published author at the age of forty, fifteen years after my first half-hearted attempt to sell my novel in Shetland. In the meantime, I had been wholly engrossed in being a mother and I felt that was my life's work.

I'm sure having children was part of my destiny, and it has definitely been by far the best and most important thing in my life. But learning to be a mother meant I often felt out of my depth. I felt I wasn't so much playing to my strengths as continuously having to develop new resources in myself.

Becoming a mother was a great adventure in uncharted waters; coming back to writing was like coming home to myself. I thought, 'This is what I was born to do.'

The idea of personal destiny is central to many myths and legends. If the hero strays from their soul's purpose, life will bring them back to the path. When they feel thwarted from what they want, life may actually be acting out of its own necessity.

Of course, if the hero is ill-fated or 'star-crossed', life may not be benign, pushing them back on the path to their own inevitable tragedy rather than helping them towards their greatest triumph.

In classical myths, people consulted the oracle to try and find out their fate, so that they might be able to alter it if it was terrible, but even the gods had little power to change what was destined to be. A famous example is in the story *Oedipus Rex*.

In this story Laius, the king of Thebes, was told by an oracle that his baby son, Oedipus, would one day kill him. Laius tried to cheat fate by piercing the baby's feet and abandoning him on a rocky mountainside, but a shepherd found him and took pity.

The shepherd gave Oedipus to Polybus and Merope, the king and queen of Corinth, and Oedipus grew up believing them to be his natural parents. Therefore, when he himself was told by the oracle that his fate was to kill his father and marry his mother, he left Corinth and vowed never to return.

On the road, he fell into an argument which ended with

him killing a man. He journeyed on and eventually arrived in Thebes, where he married the recently widowed queen, Iocasta. They lived together for many years and had several children.

When the city was struck by a terrible plague, Oedipus again consulted the oracle, to find out what was causing it. Gradually the truth was revealed, that the man he had killed on the highway was his natural father, Laius, and the woman he had married, being Laius's widow, was his natural mother.

Laius had failed to cheat fate, and so had his son, Oedipus. What drives their story forward to its conclusion is not, as in the hero's journey, what the hero wants, but the inescapable pull of the fate that awaits him.

In this writing exercise, we are going to shift the perspective from the hero to their destiny. Rather than building the story from what the hero wants, as in the hero's quest, we'll start from what life wants, and tell the story of how it brings them back to their true path.

Writing what life wants

The story starts with the protagonist's destiny moment and then backtracks to show how they got there. This is quite a common device in novels, where the reader knows at the outset how the story will finish, so the question which engages their interest isn't 'What will happen in the end?' but 'How did that ending come about?'

More obviously than usual, this kind of story makes a perfect circle, returning to where it first began.

The destiny moment

Your protagonist's destiny moment will not necessarily be their death, but the crowning moment of their life, in which we understand their quintessential Self and see their full potential realised.

It may be something on the grand scale, which defines a career in public life, such as Martin Luther King's 'I have a dream' speech, or Enoch Powell's 'rivers of blood'; Margaret Thatcher's triumph in the Falklands, or Tony Blair's ill-fated war in Iraq; Anthony Gormley's *Angel of the North*, or Tracy Emin's bed.

It may be an unlikely second destiny moment, after your protagonist appears to have already fulfilled their potential in another field, such as the cricketer Imran Khan becoming a prominent politician, or the 'sex-kitten' Brigitte Bardot, a high-profile animal rights campaigner.

Of course, not everyone is born to greatness; Life wants ants as well as elephants, daisies as well as towering pines. It wants witnesses as well as performers, followers as well as gurus, foot soldiers as well as generals.

Your protagonist may not be born for greatness, but they were born to fulfil a purpose, and will still have their destiny moment. It may be their diamond wedding anniversary, surrounded by three generations of family, or reaching their target amount in fund-raising for a charity close to their heart, or making a break for freedom after a lifetime of being beaten down.

Will your protagonist's destiny moment be a triumph

or a tragedy? Life wants victims and villains as well as conquering heroes. Without Judas, Jesus could not have achieved his destiny moment on the cross.

So decide what your protagonist is like, and what their crowning moment will be, and write some notes. Remember, this isn't about trying to write something 'good'. It's experimental, like all the writing tasks in this book, and it's experiential – the idea is to use writing as a means of experiencing, in imagination, what it feels like if, as well as nature and nurture, you put the pull of destiny into the mix.

Take about ten minutes to write the scene of your protagonist's destiny moment.

The push and pull to the finish line

Now go back and tell the story of how your protagonist came to their destiny moment. The tension in the narrative will come from the protagonist's reluctance or refusal to follow the path life wants for them.

Say your protagonist's fate is to hang himself in a prison cell after being exposed as a child molester. He may have tried to stall or deny his fate by being an exceptionally respectable figure in his community, or taking holy orders. In that situation, you can see how easily life could have pulled him back to his path by putting temptation in his way.

He may retreat into self-delusion and actually believe himself to be a friend to vulnerable children. He may try to avoid detection or, when caught, to deny all charges. But life will deliver him to his destiny at last.

What if your protagonist's fate is a fortuitous one?

Maybe she is destined to build her own business and become a leading philanthropist, the kind of destiny you might expect her to embrace. Why might she resist?

Maybe when the opportunity comes to start a business, she feels she isn't clever or brave enough to take it. Or she might take it, but then lack the confidence to build it up. So Life gives her a little push – her husband loses his job, and her fledgling business needs to make more money.

Reluctantly, she invests their life savings in expanding her business, but then she feels guilty about going on with it because it's starting to impact upon her family life. And so the push and pull goes on, until her crowning moment, receiving her OBE from the Queen.

The point about a person's destiny is that the gods know what it is, but the mere mortal doesn't, just as, in a novel, the author knows but the protagonist doesn't. In the case of this shape of story, the author and the reader know, but the protagonist has no idea what Life has in store for them.

There may come a point when the protagonist understands and embraces their destiny, fully accepting that this is what they were always meant to do or be. Or there may come a point when they understand it but put up one final act of resistance.

When you are planning the rest of the story, even if you don't want to start at the very beginning when your protagonist was a little child, take a few moments to imagine them in their childhood home. See the acorn in them, which carries the pattern of their future.

What is it about their nature – their unusual gift,

their fatal flaw – which bears the spark for their fate? How does the way they relate to the people around them foreshadow their future in the world?

As you guide them on their path, pulling them back when they stray, be as inventive as you like. Life itself is inventive. Who would think that twenty-seven years of lonely incarceration might have lead to Nelson Mandela becoming the first ever democratically elected President of South Africa?

Think of classical myths where fate plays a hand – they always have plenty of unlikely twists and turns. Shakespeare's story of the 'star-crossed lovers', Romeo and Juliet, is a fine example, with Juliet taking the poison which will make her appear to have died, the messenger failing to deliver this information to Romeo, Romeo finding Juliet apparently dead and procuring poison for himself, and so on.

It doesn't matter how you get your protagonist to their destiny moment; just enjoy the power you have, as the author of their fate, to help or force them to it.

Take about half an hour to write the rest of the story.

In Martin Amis's novel, *Time's Arrow*, the whole story is told in reverse. It begins with the protagonist's death and then tracks back, scene by scene, to his beginning.

When you have written your story, you could play with it, re-ordering the scenes so that instead of starting at the end and then telling the story from the beginning to that point, you tell it completely in reverse, starting at the end and ending at the beginning.

That might be an interesting experiment.

As people were long mistaken about the motion of the sun, so they are even yet mistaken about the motion of that which is to come. The future stands firm... but we move in infinite space.

Rainer Maria Rilke

The fact that dreams can be predictive is another reason why we shouldn't be too rigidly fixed on the notion that we can always interpret them. But, a word of warning, you really can't tell which dreams are predictive except in retrospect.

If you find, on rereading old diaries, that some of your dreams have foretold specific situations and events, don't freak yourself out by worrying every time you have a bad dream in case it might come true.

In a lifetime of dreaming, you may have enough unmistakably predictive dreams to make a convincing case for the possibility of prediction, but the actual number is likely to be very small.

Simply accepting that it might be possible to predict the future throws into doubt all our ideas about time, by which we understand our own lives and the world around us.

We already know that the past is unreliable. Research into how memory works has shown that it's a story which changes and evolves in the light of the present moment, because new experiences have to be assimilated and become part of a coherent whole. People may even 'remember' things which never happened, if those things feel likely within the context of the rest of their memories.

The possibility of prediction shows our ideas about the future are unreliable too. We think it doesn't exist, except in hopes, fears and fantasies, and that it therefore hasn't played a part in shaping who we are. But if at least some moments in the future are already written, that re-opens an old door from pre-scientific, pre-psychological eras – the notion of personal destiny.

If we accept the idea of personal destiny, then the task is to find out what Life requires of us. It's an attitude of co-operation and flow. We still have to follow our own ambitions and desires, like the hero on the hero-quest, but in the knowledge that Life may have other, more important plans. It's the attitude of Jesus on the cross. Take this cup away from me – yet not as I will, but as You will.

It can be difficult to accept that there may be a call of destiny, but if you engage with life from this perspective, meeting your blocks and challenges as well as your joys and triumphs as things that are somehow meant to be, you align with something far bigger than yourself, and can move forward without fear. As Joan of Arc is reported to have said, 'I am not afraid... I was born to do this.'

Of course, even if you let go of conventional ideas about it, you still have to understand the concept of time and live 'as if', because that's how the world works. I have written the memoir part of this book as if the events happened in a step-by-step way, in order to create a coherent narrative.

Everything I have reported here did happen, including all the dreams, exactly as I originally recorded them, but they didn't all happen in this order. Dreams, being products emerging from the unconscious, are always ahead of understanding. You may feel their significance immediately, like a light-bulb moment, but on the other hand it can take years, until you have more knowledge in place from other sources, before you can assimilate it.

The custard cream dream, for example, happened very early on, when I was still living in Shetland. It did have an immediate effect on me, starting me thinking about the nature of matter and the material world, but I didn't fully feel the effect until I began to study Zen. It was as if the dream put down a marker which led me in that direction.

The archetypes were also on the move much earlier than I've reported here, but I didn't understand them as such at the time of dreaming. I barely noticed that some of my dream characters were nameless or faceless ones, and I certainly had no concept of the universal human template giving form and energy to my personal stories and images.

The dreams happened in chronological order along the timeline of my life, but the learning followed on various timelines of its own, as if the dreams were seeds with different germination times.

What matters in a memoir is the development of the theme, rather than the chronology of events, and so I've unhooked the dreams from the timeline and reorganised them to follow the unfolding of my understanding instead.

In life, as in fiction, the direction and momentum of flow is much wider and deeper than the linear concept of time. Time isn't a thread, but a living fabric, with different strands which move at different paces.

But just because time, as we understand it, may not be

the underlying structure on which experience is built, that does not mean there isn't any structure at all. There is structure, only we can't see it beneath the rational model we impose upon it.

We have to stop focusing hard on the thread and take a step back if we want to see the whole fabric, rippling and shifting like the sea.

3 The Cloths of Heaven

Synchronicities are little miracles through which an
otherwise Unseen Consciousness communicates with
us. We may speak to the gods in prayer, but significant
coincidence is the medium whereby they speak to us.

Frank Joseph

If you make sense of experience by looking for cause-
and-effect links between what happened in the past,
what's going on today and what's likely to happen in the
future, you build a coherent narrative on a line of time,
but that line is all you can see.

It's like the blue game, where you ask people to look
around for a few minutes and spot all the blue things they
can see. Then you ask them to close their eyes and tell
you all the yellow things they saw... and they can't do it.
The blue game demonstrates that you only see what you
are looking for.

As soon as you stop looking for cause-and-effect links
on a line of time, you notice other links, things which are
meaningfully connected, yet in a non-causal way. Jung
called this 'synchronicity'.

For example, a friend of mine was upset because she
couldn't get to her sister's funeral in Uganda, but on the
day, at the time of the service, she went into the little

Oxfordshire chapel where she was staying, to say her own goodbye.

The chapel was deserted, but on the table just inside the door she found a cap with a picture of an elephant on it, and flipping it over, found a label inside which said 'Made in Africa'.

We normally shrug off incidents of synchronicity as 'just a coincidence', the way a player of the blue game will have skimmed over the yellow things, but if we stop and take note, we begin to see more and more of them, until they feel less like one-offs and more like the actual fabric of life.

Years ago, a solicitor friend of mine was sitting in his office pondering on how he might personally mark the millennium, when he hit upon the idea of cycling round the world. He decided to research how to go about it. Stepping outside to get some lunch, he saw a book lying open on the pavement. He picked it up. It was a book about cycling around the world.

That experience freaked him out, but it also made him alert to the possibility of meaningful coincidence. He began to experience more and more synchronicitous events, particularly through crosswords and puzzles.

One time, on a visit, he was doing his crossword, when I mentioned that Einstein was reputed to have said there were two ways you could look at life – one, believing that everything was a miracle and the other, that nothing was. But if you actually thought about it, there was really only one.

My friend folded his newspaper, and there on the bottom of the page, the quote for the day was, '"There are two ways to live: you can live as if nothing is a miracle; you can live as if everything is a miracle" – Albert Einstein.'

He later emailed me other examples, such as this one: 'There was an ad on TV for a Justin Timberlake album. He doesn't interest me so why I remarked to J that he once had a backing group called NSync, I don't know. But that came up the very next day in the newspaper quiz.'

In other emails he talked about dinner-party topics of conversation which had shown up in his crossword the next day, adding, 'These are so frequent now... they have become the norm.'

When I do a session on synchronicity in my workshops, people always have something to report that's happened during the week. For example, someone volunteering at a nearby National Trust property was chatting to visitors who remarked that it was just like a tiny hamlet they knew in Kent – which happened to be the village she was born in. Someone else was filing applications at work when the phone rang, and it was the man whose application she had just completed.

These 'meaningful coincidences' can also link to dreams. My solicitor friend, for example, dreamt that he fell asleep in the front row at a production of Ibsen's *A Doll's House*. The next night, he had dinner with some people who had just been to see the play, although he hadn't even realised it was on.

A workshop participant reported a dream about a ring like one she had had when she was young. It was a common design at that time. It wound round and round your finger like a snake, and had a snake's head. 'You never see them these days,' she said. The next day she texted to tell me she had just come across one on a stall in a local flea market.

On one occasion, a participant's dream sparked off

synchronicities across the group. She dreamt, 'everyone is eating glass bowls of pink ice cream'. At the next session someone reported a synchronicity that she had just met a man here in Cornwall who, it turned out, worked in London selling ice creams outside Embankment Station; she had bought an ice cream from his stall the previous week.

This led someone else to remark that she had just returned a book she had borrowed, about ice-cream selling in Gibraltar, and then a third person said her husband had been sailing that week with a friend who owned a local ice cream factory.

It's not at all surprising to us if someone dreams about something that's come up in their waking life; the surprising thing is when it's the other way around. This is things manifesting in waking life which have first come up in dreams.

Synchronicity is the outer world reflecting and responding to the inner. Tuning into it is like tuning into dreams in that something you may have barely noticed before is suddenly revealed, and it's a vibrant, magical, omnipresent aspect of everyday life.

Simply becoming aware of these patterns of non-causal connections brings a sense of richness, mystery and secret meaning. It suggests an 'Unseen Consciousness' or organising principle at work in the world, and it's personal. It reflects and responds to your personal thoughts and dreams.

Awareness alone is enough to bring the magic; working with the 'Unseen Consciousness' brings power. You may ask for signs and portents, to help you make decisions or gain information. You may seek and receive affirmation in your endeavours.

To the modern mind, this idea sounds like ignorant superstition, and it's possible you may be experiencing a strong reaction against it. But superstition is defined as, 'A belief, practice, or rite irrationally maintained by ignorance of the laws of nature.'

We don't live in the dark ages now, and we are definitely not irrational or ignorant of the laws of nature. The experience of synchronicity, in a post-scientific age, is an extra. It doesn't replace or negate the rational approach, but expands upon it.

Understanding that there is more to life than what we can rationally comprehend is like understanding there is more to dreams than what we can interpret.

Perceiving these patterns of non-causal connections shows us the limitations of the rational approach, and therefore enables us to use it more wisely, just as creative dreaming offers a wider context for interpretation which enables us to know when it is appropriate, why it isn't always appropriate and how to avoid misunderstandings and mistakes.

Far from undermining our respect for the power of reason and our knowledge of the laws of nature, the experience of synchronicity, like every mind-expanding experience, also shows us the value of keeping both feet firmly grounded in the certainties of science and reason.

Embracing the mysterious patterns of synchronicity means grounding yourself in a wider, deeper and more 'real' reality. It brings the external world into balance with psyche, and that is a kind of completion.

Deliberately merging the dream reality with the reality of waking life, says Carlos Castaneda, is what sorcerers call 'completing the energy body'.

I was walking in a landscape, and everything was talking to me – sticks, stones, grass, earth, leaves...

When I was writing my dream book as an autobiography, all that thinking about my life made me start to notice weird patterns. The title, 'Pink Jacket', came from a picture I had painted to encourage myself in my first steps as a published author.

Rereading my dream diaries, I saw a link with one of my earliest recorded dreams, about the jacket my mother made for me out of strawberries, and subsequent dreams which referred back to it.

Looking through old photos, I found my oldest child's first school portrait, and remembered I had sewn a little strawberry onto the front of her pinafore, because I couldn't bear to see her dressed all in dreary grey and blue. These links had been completely unconscious at the time.

My daughter in her strawberry dress

254

Another pattern was around my birth and the births of my daughters. I had got to the bottom of the knifeman dreams through the astrologer telling me, 'One of the most important things in your life happened about six weeks before you were born.' This was my big sister falling into a coma, being in hospital and starting her life as a diabetic, with everything that meant to the family I was born into.

My older daughter was born six weeks before her due date, and six weeks before my younger daughter's due date I developed a medical problem which complicated the rest of the pregnancy and presented a serious risk to both of us.

Thinking about due dates, my first child was due on 22nd August – 22.8. The number which had come up in my dreams from the start, it still did and still does today. Had she slotted in with my pattern, but then chosen her own moment?

Glimpsing these patterns made me rethink other things I'd previously dismissed as just 'odd'. For example, when the children were young we used to go camping for three or four weeks every summer.

One year, my watch stopped working after a day or two under canvas, so I bought a new battery, but it still didn't work. When we got home, it spontaneously started working again.

The same thing happened the following year – my watch stopped when we went on holiday, I bought a new battery, but it didn't start working again until we got home.

If I hadn't loved that watch so much – it had a sun and a moon which moved through different phases throughout the day – I would have thrown it away, because it seemed to have become unreliable. It was only on the third year it stopped on holiday that I realised that was the only time it stopped – it wasn't unreliable during the rest of the year.

After that, I stopped worrying about it, or buying batteries as soon as it packed up. It was completely weird, but it seemed as if my watch was just taking a holiday too.

When I was learning the tarot cards, I used to choose one every morning, and then contemplate upon it during the day. I had noticed that I sometimes dreamt about a particular card, only to draw it from the pack the next morning.

Now, I realised how odd that was. I mean, if I'd drawn a card and then dreamt about it, that wouldn't be surprising at all – dreams often echoed bits and pieces from the day world. But how could the cards, in waking life, reflect something I had dreamt the night before? There are seventy-eight cards in a standard pack – to draw the one you dreamt about was an extraordinary coincidence.

Then there were waking premonitions – I knew it was possible to have a dream which predicted an event, but how could real life imitate what was going to happen?

My youngest child was knocked down by a car when she was in her teens. As soon as I got the call, I remembered three days previously, driving into town, I had seen a teenage girl walking along the verge of the main road. She was too close to the traffic and I was afraid she might get run over.

Drawing closer, I thought this girl actually was my daughter, and my heart leapt to my throat. I slowed to get a better look and, seeing it wasn't her, told her to be careful, and drove on, feeling really unsettled.

All these odd experiences from my past made me wonder, was it possible that the waking world could reflect and respond to a person's inner life, those imaginative processes, stories and images, past and future memories, which go on beneath the surface whether we're sleeping or awake?

I started to be alert to synchronicity in my daily life, to try and notice when it happened, and capture those instances before they got the 'that's odd' label slapped on them and were forgotten.

It was like when I first began to recall and record my dreams. As soon as I set my dial to notice my synchronicities, they were everywhere and all the time, not sporadic instances but a continuous and abundant flow; not only big single, memorable events, but multiple small ones.

I might bump into someone I hadn't seen for ages, just when I happened to be thinking about them, or be given a book by a friend which had just been recommended to me by someone else.

One time, when I was feeling down, a friend gave me a hardback A4 notebook and a matching loose-leaf folder, as a random cheer-up present. She didn't know that I used A4 notebooks for my dream diaries, let alone that I had finished my current one that very morning. Neither did she know that I always bought a new loose-leaf file when I was starting a new book, and I had just signed a contract that very afternoon.

At first, I simply noticed these synchronicities; I was an observer, as I had been when I was coming new to dreams. But this gradually changed. It became interactive. I began to feel that life was actually communicating with me.

Often, the outer world seemed to be making an unmistakable response to an inner dilemma. When that happened, I didn't generally try to interpret, although sometimes, as in dreams, the meaning seemed immediately clear.

For example, one winter afternoon, I was sitting outside feeling very troubled because, after more than thirty years, I knew my marriage was effectively over, but I didn't want to admit it to myself.

I was in a very lonely place. But as I sat there, a big dragonfly flew past my face with a whirr of wings and landed on the wall beside my head. I turned to look at him. He was iridescent blue, so beautiful, and so odd, in the middle of November.

The dragonfly let me look at him for a long moment, then fluttered down and rested in the palm of my hand, as if to say, 'Yes, see, I really am here – you aren't imagining it!'

The strangeness of this encounter, in a time of emotional turmoil, felt like life reassuring me, although I didn't try to interpret it any more than that. I didn't consider whether the dragonfly had any symbolic significance.

A few weeks later, when things had reached crisis point, I was standing by the window in the middle of the night, gazing out. The moon was full, and moonlight lit the garden and the fields beyond. I saw a sudden furious movement in the hedge. It stopped, but then happened again. I tied my dressing gown round me and went to investigate.

Behind the trees and bushes along the side of the garden, the farmer had a wire fence to keep his stock in. A big ram had got his head stuck through the wire. When he saw me, he burst into a frenzy of tugging and pulling, trying to get himself free. I waited.

He stopped struggling, and looked at me, his eyes bulging and terrified. I stepped forward and prised the wires apart, feeling his breath on my hands, hearing the noise of it on the still air. He pulled himself free and backed away, but then he just stood there looking at me, in the cold light of the moon.

I thought, 'The ram is my animal – I am an Aries. He was trapped, and he needed to be free.' It was like waking from a dream with that feeling of, 'Aha – I know what that means.'

But, as with dreams, I was wary of being gullible or imagining what I wanted to see. I would never make a major decision on the strength of something which felt like a sign, so it was still a long time before I finally found myself living in a rented barn conversion, on my own.

The first year of my new life was the last year of Anne's, and we spoke on the phone more often. She was a very intuitive person, and she and I had an intuitive connection. She was too ill to come and see me in the new place, but when we first spoke on the phone after I moved there, she said, 'I don't know why, but I seem to have a picture in my mind of you with a red settee and a Victorian-style lace curtain.'

She laughed, because she knew I wasn't a lace curtains kind of person. But she was right. There were lace curtains in that house, which I hadn't got round to taking down yet, although I hated them, and I had just bought a new red settee.

Anne was talking about her death by then, and I went up to Shetland to visit her one last time, to say goodbye. Other people I'd known with cancer had lost a lot of their body-weight in the last months, and hardly looked like themselves any more. But Anne still had the soft plumpness of her skin and her beautiful smile.

She was in bed, but not in too much discomfort to talk. She had grown up in a spiritualist family, so she believed that people who died simply passed to 'the other side', where the living could still make contact with them. I asked her to visit me afterwards. 'Come and see me,' I said. 'I won't be afraid.'

A few months later, she died. I fully expected her to come, as my sister had done, and later my mother-in-law, ghostly visitations in the night, but time went by and there was no sign of her. One morning, pulling back the lace curtain, which I still hadn't got around to removing, I suddenly thought of Anne.

'You never visited me,' I said.

The postman put some letters through the door. One of them was addressed to 'Miss Anne Robertson'. It was Anne's name. I had never received mail addressed to that name before, and I guessed it must be a former tenant from a long time previously, as I had forwarding addresses for the most recent two.

It was a strange coincidence, this letter arriving the very day that I told Anne off for not visiting me. In fact, it felt so strange, it had to be a fluke. I wrote 'not known at this address' on the envelope and put it back in the post.

The following week, the postman delivered two new letters on the same day, both addressed to Miss Anne Robertson. It felt like she was saying, 'Yes, this is me. You asked me to visit, so stop ignoring me!' I sent her a big thank you, and I never received another letter addressed to Anne Robertson after that.

These signs and omens came thick and fast, the more that I took notice of them. I couldn't tell whether they had always been there and I simply hadn't seen them, or whether there really were more of them, and life was speaking up now because I had started to listen.

I had a dream which fell into three parts. It reminded me of the Zen teaching about the de-symbolisation of the world, 'When you first study Zen…' which I've quoted here at the beginning of my chapter titled 'Weightlessness'.

In the first part, I was walking in a landscape, and there were sticks and twigs all around, and they were all like mobile phones, talking to me, and I to them.

In the second part, I was walking in the same landscape and the sticks and twigs were mobile phones, and I was picking them up and having lots of conversations with them.

In the last part, I was walking in the same landscape, and

everything was talking to me – sticks, stones, grass, earth, leaves...

It was a small step from listening to actually asking for specific information, like the step from realising that dreams could contain information about waking life to incubating them for the purpose of answering a question – am I pregnant? Is this symptom serious?

As in dreams, the answers always came quickly: a sudden rainbow above the road, a baby woodpecker on the windowsill. I would take note, but always trust my judgement about the decisions and directions I thought I should take.

The difference was that now I had more feeling of flow. If life supported me, making things easy, and the omens felt good, then that was affirming, and it gave me more confidence in what I was doing.

If I kept meeting one block after another and the omens felt bad, I would stop and take stock. But the decision whether to press forward or not was always based on my assessment of the situation, rather than any signs and portents.

The medium I mostly used for asking for information was the tarot. I had known it worked, ever since I started studying the cards years before, but I hadn't properly clocked how and why.

Now, it felt clearer to me. You got the cards which answered your enquiry through synchronicity, the external reality of the tarot reflecting and responding to your inner world.

In my writing, I was using collage-making long before I started teaching it. Like with tarot, I would hold my enquiry softly in my mind as I flicked through the magazines – What is this character like? What is the main thrust of the story? What would be a good title?

I knew it worked – you always found the images, colours, words and patterns you needed in order to find the answer – but now I felt I was beginning to understand how. This, also, was synchronicity, and I could use the technique with even greater confidence, fuelled by the feeling of flow.

In those first few years after my marriage broke down I had to try lots of new things because I was worried about making enough money to live on and some of my initiatives flowed much better than others.

As well as my usual steady stream of commissions for things like educational CD-ROMs, magazine articles and little books such as Rabbittalk *and* Finding Fizz *I tried my hand at reading for a literary consultancy, only to find that it took me a huge amount of time for very little financial reward.*

I decided to start again with my dream book, this time as a work of straight non-fiction, because I was in the zone having just done a major rewrite of my adult bullying book for a new publisher. I planned to back this new dream book up with research based on teaching some workshops, but both projects ran aground on a rocky shore of difficulties and disappointments.

When it came to the book, I started by reading some of the latest titles on dreams and rereading the ones I had found most interesting two decades before, in order to be able to write footnotes and make exact attributions.

But the process soon started to feel stifling and un-creative. I wasn't interested in unravelling the fine detail of other people's theories and arguments in order to construct my own case in relation to theirs. I wasn't interested in theories at all – I was interested in experience, and particularly the mind-blowing experiences that could come from opening to dreams.

When it came to the dream workshops, several people dropped out at the very last minute, there were big problems with the venue and I lost my nerve over the content, opting to follow the well-trodden path of interpretation rather than creative dreaming.

So after these false starts I decided to stick to my home base of children's writing, and at that time publishers were really only looking for one thing – series fiction. I chanced upon a session at a conference of children's writers which gave me precise information about how to pitch and write a fiction series.

For my first try, I deliberately chose to write for a younger age group because the books are shorter and I thought that would mean a better financial return for time spent.

My first series, 'Car-mad Jack', was Highly Recommended in the Red House Children's Book Awards but sadly got very little promotion, because the person who commissioned it left before it went to press.

When that happens, a book can fall between the cracks, because the new publisher wants to develop projects of their own, and your abandoned book has no one in-house to champion its cause. But they did encourage me. 'You really can write fiction,' they said, inviting me to submit some ideas for a new series.

This time I decided to write for older children. Writing longer fiction would give me more room to develop my characters and weave in lots of subplots, rather than having to stick to the kind of simple, single plotline that a five-year-old could follow.

I knew from trying to write my autobiography, that life wasn't a tidy line of events. It was a pattern of themes and characters, plots and subplots, twists and coincidences; of past, present and future, all interwoven.

It was a fabric with a scattering of strong images that stood out from the rest – a dusty ditch, a dead rat, a dancing ballerina. Threads and specks of pink, a jacket, a strawberry. Patches of *brilliant aquamarine. An iridescent fleck of dragonfly.*

The new series was called 'By Peony Pinker'. It was a Blue Peter Book Club selection, and sold well overseas. I only recently noticed, because one of my sons pointed it out, that having abandoned 'Pink Jacket', I wrote the 'pink' into Peony Pinker and the 'jacket' into 'Car-mad Jack'.

Because I really enjoyed these forays into fiction series, I began to work on yet another new version of my dream book, this time as fiction. I was excited by the idea of creating a protagonist whose life events, settings and characters would have nothing in common with mine, yet who would experience the same kind of adventures in dreaming.

My first working title for my dream-book-as-fiction was 'Pomegranate'. It was harder than I had anticipated, planning something so much longer than the children's fiction I was used to, and I spent a lot of days just walking around, playing with ideas in my mind.

During this planning period, when I was wondering whether I really wanted to commit, I visited a holy well. There were coins pressed into the walls, ribbons and little crystals, all the usual offerings. But also, big and solid, incongruous as a red tennis ball, someone had left a pomegranate, perched on a protruding stone.

In my writing, as in my personal life at this turbulent time of transition, I felt supported by my growing sense of an organising principle behind everything, this all-knowing, all-seeing presence which could hear and respond to my questions and prayers.

This web of secret knowledge, wisdom and power, which was more than a name or an idea of God; it was the actual experience of God in the world.

If we pay attention to our dreams, instead of living in a cold, impersonal world of meaningless chance, we may begin to emerge into a world of our own, full of important and secretly ordered events.

Marie-Louise von Franz

You can use the fact that the external world may reflect and respond to a person's inner life very effectively in fiction. Coincidences in the plot can delight and surprise readers without necessarily feeling implausible. Signs and omens can bring a frisson of mystery and anticipation.

Making the weather or setting reflect the mood of the protagonist intensifies the emotion in the scene, for example, King Lear's madness as he rages in the thunderstorm.

Pathetic fallacy can add intensity as well, attributing emotions to inanimate objects: 'the sad neglected garden', 'the brooding trees', 'the angry clouds', 'the flowers dancing in the breeze.'

You can try using some of these techniques in the following exercise.

The revelation

Here, you are not writing a whole story but just a scene, so you don't have to reach a resolution for your character. You are just writing up to a turning point.

a) Choose an emotion, and complete this sentence – 'Someone is feeling...'

b) Who are they? Make notes on your character – their name, age, appearance, personality. Why are they feeling happy/anxious/angry/whatever?

c) Where are they? Make some notes on the setting, particularly how the weather, time of day and environment might reflect their emotional state. Jot down ideas for pathetic fallacy.

d) What is the significant object or omen which challenges, changes or affirms the way they are feeling? It might be something which breaks a low mood with a glimmer of brightness, or a happy one with a sudden sense of foreboding.

You aren't looking for a supernatural or fantasy object, but some aspect of ordinary life which magically reveals something to the character and affects how they are feeling.

For example, if your character is feeling indecisive, maybe glimpsing some words on a billboard or overhearing a chance remark or seeing something which reminds them of a relevant past experience, might make them suddenly know what to do.

If they are feeling happy, a brutal moment in nature such as a hawk swooping down on a sparrow might shock them out of it. If anxious, the sound of music nearby might distract them from their worry.

e) Write the scene. Try to convey how your character is feeling through your description of the setting, and end with the moment of revelation or transformation.

Using settings and plot points that reflect and amplify the inner world of your protagonist is particularly effective if you reserve it for the big scenes, when you really want to make an impact.

> ... it is not necessary to acquire a conviction about something if you have experienced it. I do not believe I have just eaten dinner. If I have had the experience, I know it. And so with recognising the difference between religious belief and religious experience.
>
> June Singer

Awareness of synchronicity as an integral part of everyday life unsettles the illusion of separateness between the inner and outer worlds. It is an experience of mystery, a movement into soul.

Synchronicity suggests an organising principle at work in the world which is mysteriously connected to the patterns of the individual psyche. It defies all human laws, and therefore when you fully acknowledge it, it is an awesome revelation.

This is religious experience, as opposed to theory. You know it exists because you can see and feel it at work in your life, the same way you know if you have eaten dinner – it happened, and now you feel full. You don't have to explain it to yourself or convince anyone else.

Angeles Arrien – my favourite writer on the tarot – says she believes an old-fashioned word for synchronicity is 'grace'. Grace is mysterious or divine intervention.

Atheist, agnostic or church goer – you don't have to be a believer in order to uncover the mysterious connections between your small self and the organising power at work in the world.

God, Goddess, Life, Spirit, Nature...You can give it any name you want to, or no name at all. It is an experience of wonder and connectedness, and if you feel it, that is grace.

The Return

When the state of dreaming has dawned, do not lie in ignorance like a corpse. Enter the natural sphere of unwavering attentiveness. Recognise your dreams, and transform illusion into luminosity.

Tibetan Buddhist prayer

Most of us are barely aware of our dream life; we may not even believe we dream at all. When dreams break through, we don't know what to do with them. We shrug them off, explain them away or take them to therapy. We keep that 'door of perception' tightly shut.

If we treat dreams in this way, we are 'lying like a corpse' – staying fixed in an unbalanced, partial and narrow position, where reality is completely defined by rational constructs and the evidence of the senses.

We are subduing the dream in the same way as we subdue the waking world, reducing it to a narrative we can understand, but the narrative is an explanation rather than a truth – not facts, but ideas and illusions.

If we engage with the dream on its own terms, we are entering a realm of experience ruled by the imagination and emotions, where reason and the senses hold no sway.

Here, meaning is not fixed, but fluid; an abundant flow of stories, symbols and images. All is movement, possibility, colour, energy, insight; illusion is transformed into luminosity.

This experience spills over into our waking life because, like Persephone returning from the Underworld, we are changed by it. We have known something different, which we cannot then un-know.

We return rebalanced, able and requiring to live more imaginatively and creatively. Where we might previously have thought of creativity as art, literature and music, an area of life closed to most adults except as consumers, now we know every moment of every life is a creation and every person a creator.

Great thinkers rate imagination more highly than intellect, yet most of us dismiss the spontaneous products of imagination, dreams and daydreams, as meaningless and without value; and although we hold certain creative works in high esteem, we box them off as a reserve for the few, and put a market value on them.

If a person travels further into imaginary realms, they may see ghosts, fairies, visions in their waking life, such as William Blake's vision of a tree filled with angels, 'bright angelic wings bespangling every bough like stars.' We label them as mad. Yet signs and visions can underpin a life of worldly success and achievement.

Blake famously journeyed into visionary realms throughout his life, but he also created his own printing method, as well as a body of astonishing artwork and creative writing, and that order of achievement requires a strong ego and a thorough grounding in 'real' life.

You can venture as far as you want to into the dream-world quite safely, so long as you stay grounded in this one. However far you go, you must always come back. The dream isn't instead of 'real' life – it's more of real life. A larger reality.

If all you do is cross the threshold, pass the beast in the basement and enter the echoing chamber of objects, where you first hear the voice of the dream, you will bring back a great treasure.

If you cross the bridge of the emotions into the landscape where dreamers meet, and walk with gods and angels; if you break through the mirror of the Shadow where ideas of self fragment, there is even greater treasure to be had.

But there is more. In *The Art of Dreaming*, Carlos Castaneda talks about the goal of seeing the energetic fabric of the world. It takes practice and dedication, but if you pay full attention to what is rather than what theoretically ought to be, then matter melts into light, and time is like a washing-line, starting nowhere, ending in nothing, strung out across the luminous darkness of space.

I'm standing still, so still – and dreams are swirling around me, some distant and some close, bright and shiny...

By the time I wrote 'Car-mad Jack' and 'By Peony Pinker' we had sold the big family house and bought two smaller ones, starting on the final straight towards divorce. At first, my new shed was full of boxes and bags that we had put up in the attic years before and forgotten about.

They stayed in my shed, gathering dust, forgotten about again, until one Saturday when I was going to a discussion evening on the topic of diaries with a group of friends.

I thought it was quite possible that amongst the boxes and bags, I might have kept some of my diaries, going right back to when I was about eight. So, that Saturday morning, I turned out my shed.

I found the diaries in a plastic case, but stuffed in with them, something I had not remembered ever putting into storage, a fat parcel of old letters from Susan, and a file her last boyfriend had sent to me after she died, containing all her poems.

It took me the rest of the day to read through these diaries, letters and poems, and it was a day of revelation. They contained a whole side of Susan, and my relationship with her, that I had forgotten.

The manner of her death seemed to have blotted out everything that went before it, tainting my memory of her with its desperation and... coldness. You would have to be completely detached from everyone and everything in your life, to go right up to the edge and then step off.

But she wasn't an unhappy person. I rediscovered the upbeat side of Susan when I reread her letters. She had had lovers, smoked weed, done different jobs; she had had wonderful dreams for her future. She had wanted to have two children of her own, and adopt a rainbow family of six others from around the world.

She was a rebel; she had no time for 'cabbagey' people and the nine-to-five way of life. She wrote to me frequently, about everything, and gave me lots of sisterly advice. She loved me, although the way she left me seemed such a total abrogation of love.

In her poems, I found another side of Susan that I had completely forgotten. She believed in God. It wasn't just me – she had had that God-thing too. She talked about past lives and the things of the soul.

I remembered one time when I was about twelve or thirteen,

she asked me to write some Latin words for a song she had composed; she didn't know any Latin but I was doing it at O level. She wanted, 'Love God, because God is our father. Give glory to God, because God loves us.'

I couldn't believe that so much had slipped through my memory in the decades since her death, like water through a sieve, leaving only the lumpen fact of her suicide.

I made a note of all these rediscoveries in my journal. 'These things I want to remember, so I'm writing them down before I burn the letters and poems.'

In the late afternoon, I built a bonfire, and burned her private writings. It wasn't until I checked my calendar when I went to bed that night that I realised what day it was. It was the anniversary of her death.

The discovery of my diaries and her letters and poems brought back a vivid sense of place for me. I remembered the sights and sounds of the suburban streets I grew up in, the smell of the air, the seasons of the trees which pushed the tarmac up around their roots and dropped their blossom, pale then brown, like the city snow which so soon turned to slush.

I was writing 'Pomegranate' as a semi-autobiographical novel, keeping some of the settings and events of my own life, and changing everything else, but as that meant there was a lot of purely fictional material, I was having to adapt the dreams to fit.

I was finding this really hard to do. My own dreams were the beautiful objects I wanted to write about; my journey in dreams, the story I wanted to tell. Some of my journey would be unbelievable as fiction, so I couldn't use it anyway. For example, the day when I had seen streams of light above every car on the motorway; that's the truth, but it is too strange for fiction.

I, like many authors, had had the experience of my agent or

editor saying something was implausible when it was the only thing in the story which had actually happened in real life.

I was also frustrated by not being able to explore my thoughts and ideas about dreaming in this fictional context without slowing down the narrative. I had never been a fan of the kind of fiction that's an obvious vehicle for the author's ideas.

I loved the adventure of writing the novel; it showed me I could write adults' fiction, and that I would definitely want to do so in the future, but after several attempts, I felt that fiction wasn't the right form for my book about dreams.

So I was back to the drawing board, with no idea what to do next, and feeling I was running out of options. Someone had told me about a small community of nuns on Fetlar, one of the North Isles of Shetland, and the next time I was between contracts, I arranged to go there on retreat.

I recently discovered a pair of dreams in my diaries from several years previously, which seemed to predict this trip. In one, I dreamt, 'I go to Fetlar. I want to stay here now. It's so beautiful, wild and bleak.'

The night before that, my dream was, 'I've come to the nuns. The Mother Superior comes out of the house. She holds me. She keeps holding. "Come on," she says – and I suddenly feel everything relax, and I cry.'

Maybe, when I went to stay with the sisters, I was simply following a track already laid down from the past but at the time, I wondered what on earth I was doing there.

I didn't need peace and quiet; I lived alone. I didn't think Fetlar was the nicest part of Shetland to have a holiday. I wasn't looking for spiritual guidance and anyway, I wasn't a Christian. The only issue I seemed unable to resolve was how to write my dream book.

So on my first day I went for a walk, and asked for a sign about why I was there. I came to a small stony beach. Something caught my eye among the wet grey pebbles. It was a piece of thick green sea-glass, its sharpness and shine all ground away.

Green was for love in the world, as pink was for love in the heart. That was the first thought I had. So as I walked back towards my retreat house I pondered whether my problem with the dream book was somehow connected with love.

But I couldn't see it, so I slipped the sea-glass pebble in my pocket and asked for another sign. Approaching my retreat house from a different side, I now saw, for the first time, that there was a big wooden plaque fixed to the outside wall. It was a cross with the word 'Love' written on it in five places.

Five times love on my retreat house wall

I was ready to shrug off the coincidence but when I went into the house I found, just inside the front door, a gift from the Mother Superior. It was one of the books she had written, and its title was, For Love Alone.

I didn't know what to make of the message, but I wasn't in any doubt now that the reason for my coming here was something to do with love. Mother Mary Agnes very kindly agreed to come to my retreat house for a talk. She asked why I had come, and I said I didn't know.

I told her about my marriage break-up and all the emotional shock waves it had sent through the whole family, but we were still a strong family, bound by ties of deep affection and love. My ex-husband and I had a warm relationship with all our children, and each other.

Talking about it brought back the painful times around our break-up so sharply that I cried, and she put her arms around me. Tension I didn't even know I had been holding, the tension to be strong and keep it together, and make it all right for everyone else, melted away. I felt myself relax.

She asked me about my life now, and I told her about my dream book, how dreams had turned out to be, for me, a spiritual journey. We talked about God. I said I could never belong to an organised religion. It seemed to me that God could not be contained in a single faith, and terrible harm and cruelty had been done in the name of religion, throughout all the ages and in the present day.

Even a moderate religion such as the Church of England had to debate whether women were the spiritual equals of men, and whether gay people should have the same right as heterosexuals to express their true selves within a loving relationship.

This seemed to me a long way from what I understood to

be the spirit of Jesus. It showed that the Church preferred its own narrow, history-bound interpretation of the Bible to the true wonder and mystery of God.

She said it didn't matter how we worshipped God. God was the same, whichever route you took; God was love. I told her that for me, God was wisdom and power, and what I felt when I experienced the presence of God in my life was gratitude and awe, rather than love.

'Worshipping God is love. You can't separate it up,' she said. 'Open to it.'

I thought about this a lot, but I couldn't feel it. It troubled me. God was everywhere in my life, but not this God. What if I had got it wrong? But I was patient, open and watchful; I had been in this situation before, with my unfolding understanding of dreams. The dawning of new insights didn't mean 'this is wrong', but 'there is more'.

When I left Fetlar, I still didn't know what I had gone there for, but I felt that somehow I had found it. I felt calmer and more clear-headed; more energised and open. If it was about my dream book, I was ready to go back and start again.

It was a friend and fellow children's author, Joe Friedman, who gave me my new direction. He had just written his own book on dreams because, as well as writing for children, he's a psychotherapist with many years' experience of working on dreams with groups and individuals.

Joe said why not combine dreaming with creative writing in my book? My approach was creative rather than interpretative, and there were already so many books about dreams, it would be something a little different. I wasn't sure how this would work, but I decided to write a new series of workshops to test some ideas out.

After what felt like the failure of my ill-fated first series of dream workshops, I had to really screw up my courage. I dreamt, 'My diving teacher wants me to dive – it's Joe Friedman! I go to the deep end. I look down. The surface of the water looks a long way away. I'm not afraid of getting hurt. I'm afraid of making a fool of myself if I get the angle wrong...'

I had been teaching creative writing workshops for several years so I knew what my angle was with those. I felt confident because I was an author with a long track record. My books were my qualification. But I had no formal qualification in dreaming, and no interest in getting one.

I was also worried about whether teaching people to dream was a good idea. It could be unsettling, or even alarming for them, if I didn't provide the right information, tools and support. I had no way of guaranteeing that an open group would not attract people with mental health issues which might make it difficult to hold the creative intention; it might steer this new group, like the first one, towards the dream-road more travelled, of interpretation.

When I had written the series, but not yet started to publicise it, I had this dream, *'I've been helping at a hospital or shelter for helpless and hopeless people. The doctor or manager says I can do the work myself now. I can be a doctor. I know how to do it and I know how it's done, from being there, and watching, and learning.'*

The dream felt like God, the doctor/manager, giving me the go-ahead, and it also gave me my angle. I wasn't an academic, but I was a person of knowledge. I knew what I knew from eclectic reading and life experience and, being well into my fifties, I had had plenty of it.

I had written my bullying books from life-learning rather than academic research, as an older person offering advice to children. I could write my dream book as an elder too.

I called my workshops 'Writing in the House of Dreams'. The title made it clear they were creative rather than interpretative, and the people who signed up were mostly writers who had done workshops with me before.

The first six went so well, I devised a follow-up course called 'More writing in the House of Dreams – the landscape beyond', in which we explored the mythic and archetypal layer in our dreams and stories.

Exhilarated and heartened by the success of these two courses, I pushed the adventure further with a third one, 'Into the Dreamspace'. I wasn't sure how workshops on dream-travel, spirits and synchronicity might be received, but the group were totally up for it, and we had some wonderful evenings of dream-sharing and writing adventures.

I knew from my own experience that dreaming and writing were a marriage made in heaven, and now I felt affirmed that it didn't only work for me. I set up a new group so that I could run through the workshops again, and started to write a kind of course book on writing and dreaming, using the same title, framework and content as the courses.

Each chapter had an introduction to a particular topic, followed by a writing exercise and then some closing thoughts, which was the same format as I used in the workshops. Working with the second group, I began to realise that I could also use my own dreams in the book, the same way as I did in workshops, in order to illustrate a point.

We started every workshop with creative dream-sharing, where you treat dreams as experience for the self. You tell them as interesting anecdotes about something which has happened to *you, and listen to other people's dreams in the same way.*

There is absolutely no attempt to link dreams with the events of waking life, so you may get to know each other's dream-life quite intimately, whilst knowing virtually nothing about their day-world at all.

I could write about my dream-world in my book, drawing upon details from it to illustrate the ideas I wanted to explore, without necessarily tying it into events in my waking life. The idea made me feel really happy, because the most exciting thing for me, and the thing I wanted to share, was my own adventures in dreams.

So, as well as the essay, exercise and closing thoughts, I added a section of memoir in each chapter, sticking to my dream journey, with just enough autobiographical detail to hang it on.

I was elated because I knew I finally had the right structure for my book. When I mentioned it to my older son – who by now was well into his twenties – he remarked, 'Of course! That's the same structure you used for your children's self-help books.'

He was right. A decade before, I had developed exactly this same hybrid essay-exercise-anecdote form for children, except with lots of jokes and quizzes thrown in. I couldn't believe that I'd taken so long and been right round the houses, just to return to it now. But I didn't regret it at all.

My dream book had taught me so much about myself as an author and the processes of writing, sometimes hard lessons which I might have ducked if I hadn't been so engaged by it, and so impassioned.

From its very first version, 'Healing Symbols', in the style of nineties self-help, to 'The Dreamer's Journey' dream workbook and the autobiographical 'Pink Jacket'; from the work of non-fiction to the novel, which itself had run to several versions, I had learnt a lot about writing but also, I had learnt a great deal more. The process of the novel in particular was to bring me my most precious insight.

The earliest version, 'Pomegranate', was a first-person narrative, but that felt too close to myself. I tried re-writing it in the third person to get some distance, calling it 'Johanna's Dream', but that still felt too narrow, so I opened it out and rewrote it as the omniscient narrator.

This gave me the opportunity to comment upon the action and, as soon as I started to add some commentary, I realised that as the narrator I could have a voice, and therefore some kind of personality.

Who or what might my omniscient narrator be? As soon as I asked the question, I knew – the narrator could be Johanna's dream. The title was already perfect; its full significance would become apparent.

I began to rework the text, from the point-of-view of the dream, at first being completely ignored, then shut out with sleeping pills, then distorted by therapy. I was the context and creator of Johanna; I was her psyche and her life flowed from me, yet she was oblivious to me.

She was oblivious, but very gradually, she became aware. When she saw me, when she heard me, when she spoke to me... writing that part felt amazing. My story, as the dream, as astonishing as hers, the dreamer.

I thought, 'For the dream, the dreamer becoming aware would be like a character in a book becoming aware of the author. Imagine that!' There you are, creating your character, weaving their story, and suddenly they catch you at it. The game is changed.

Now your character can hear you, speak to you, express their desires about how they want their story to develop. They can thank you when their story is going well, and have their own ideas about how it could be better.

And you would listen to them; you would listen because you love them, and because it would be so wonderful to be known.

Writing a book is a hard and demanding task, and the outcome is unpredictable. It requires patience, dedication and attention to detail. Why does an author do it? Because of love. You couldn't go the distance unless you loved the creative process, and cared about your characters.

What if love was the reason why the dream dreams me? What if love was the reason my creator creates me? I thought about all the gifts and blessings of being in the world; of family, and nature, and all the beautiful objects of the mind and imagination.

But what about bereavements and breakdowns, despair, depression, divorce… How could a loving creator leave you to flounder in the darkness?

When I thought it, I knew how, because I was a mother. I knew that sometimes the hardest thing was to step back and allow your child to flounder. How else will he learn that he can be strong? How else will she learn that she can survive?

When you teach your child to swim, the moment comes when you have to let go. You have to stand back while he struggles, even though he's out of his element and afraid, even though he may sink under the water, because otherwise he will never know that he can swim.

If I had not been sucked down into the depths, I would not have known how to master this unfamiliar element of inner space. Each time I sank, I developed new skills and greater strength.

You don't need much skill or strength if you stay within your depth, but if you want to go further and further out from the shore, you have to be confident that you can get back.

I dreamt, 'I am walking in a forest of my dreams. All around me, holes are opening up, perfectly round holes, and they all lead down to the same place, and that is Truth, and truth comes up out of them, the one truth which is Love. It doesn't matter what the layers are in between, what the stories are.

'It wasn't always like that. The forest of dreams was once impenetrable, a dark impenetrable place, before the journey.'

Heirloom

She gave me childhood's flowers,
Heather and wild thyme,
Eyebright and tormentil,
Lichen's mealy cup
Dry on wind-scored stone,
The corbies on the rock,
The rowan by the burn.

Sea-marvels a child beheld
Out in the fisherman's boat,
Fringed pulsing violet
Medusa, sea-gooseberries,
Starfish on the sea-floor,
Cowries and rainbow-shells
From pools on a rocky shore.

Gave me her memories,
But kept her last treasure:

'When I was a lass,' she said,
'Sitting among the heather,
'Suddenly I saw
'That all the moor was alive!
'I have told no one before.'

That was my mother's tale.
Seventy years had gone
Since she saw the living skein
Of which the world is woven,
And having seen, knew all;
Through long indifferent years
Treasuring the precious pearl.

Kathleen Raine

A moment of transcendence can transform an ordinary life. It doesn't have to be a vision of angels in a tree, or light streams moving above a motorway, or a colour of indescribable beauty in a dream. It doesn't have to be an astonishing insight, such as seeing 'the living skein of which the world is woven'.

It may be the moment you were sitting in the bus shelter out of the rain, eating fish and chips with your boyfriend and you suddenly felt, 'This is perfect.' Or the moment you brought lemonade to your children playing in their paddling pool and paused, tray in hand, stopped by the sudden thought, 'This is what life is for.'

We try to create these moments, in perfect wedding days, family holidays, Christmases – snapshots of something pure and intense which will sustain us through the humdrum of every day.

If you are a contemplative kind of person, you may experience many transcendent moments, because everything is a miracle if you take the time to notice. Clouds moving across the sky; the voice of a friend; a dinner plate half-submerged in soapy water.

These moments are private and personal, because they're hard to put into words. No one else could understand how something remarkably unremarkable could suddenly light up a life.

Here's a writing exercise about capturing the magic within the mundane. I've named it after the poet's image of the pearl, that bright jewel hidden inside the living organism.

The precious pearl

Picture an ordinary area of an ordinary life. This may be a relationship, a job situation, or an environment, which is thoroughly familiar to the person, in every way.

The person may be someone you know, a character from a book/play/TV show, or one invented for this exercise.

Write a list beginning, 'It is...' or 'It was...' describing aspects of this ordinary area of an ordinary life. Set it out like a poem.

For example, supposing you were thinking of Reggie Perrin's nine-to-five:

It is the furled umbrella in the hat-stand by the door
The shoes striding time along Coleridge Close
The train, jam-packed, eleven minutes late,
Defective junction box at New Malden
It is the ugly front of Sunshine Desserts
The boss's desk, the 'Sorry, CJ...'

It doesn't have to sound poetic – you are simply drawing a sketch, capturing the flavour of the situation in a few of its objects. Play with it, like the child 'stringing beads in kindergarten'.

It doesn't have to be sad or negative, but just very familiar, like the natural world described in Kathleen Raine's poem. It's your character's ordinary world. If I were writing this about my everyday world of work, that would be a very happy place. It would be bright books, enthusiastic editors, positive reviews, emails from readers; it would be author talks and workshops, book blogs and wonderful writing friends.

But the secret pearl is this dream book, which has been there since before I was ever published. It was never attached to any promise of publication; it earned me no income; it took up half my writing time from the beginning, and slowed my output as a children's author.

Everything I've done in my career has been feeding my secret pearl. Whenever I've had an advance, I've used it to buy time for working on my dream book. All the writing skills I've developed in my children's books, the learning about the business side, marketing, self-promotion – it's all been there to feed this work.

I don't need my precious pearl to change my life because

it already has, and it continues to do so, every waking moment. It defines the writer I know I am, although to the world, I'm Jenny Alexander, children's author.

When you have got a dozen or so objects in your list, come to the precious pearl, the secret thought, experience or inspiration that your character keeps close to their heart.

For Reggie Perrin, it might be his vision of going to the beach, stripping off his pinstripe suit, and walking naked into the sea. He can bear the stultifying boredom of his life, because he has secretly seen the possibility of escape.

Start this part with something like, 'But once...' and describe the moment of insight which has given meaning to your character's situation, the secret pearl they think about when life seems meaningless or dull.

Finish your poem with a return to their present, ordinary life. Show how this secret pearl transforms their experience every day, either by making it possible for them to continue as they are, or by inspiring them to make a change.

If you are feeling brave, you might then repeat the exercise, writing about yourself, and your own precious pearl.

> To write happily and with self-trust you must discover what there is in you, this bottomless fountain of imagination and knowledge.
>
> Brenda Ueland

I'm sure one reason I have never struggled with any kind of angst or blocks about my writing is that I was a dreamer first, and therefore I already knew that there was in me, 'this bottomless fountain of imagination and knowledge'. I also knew how to engage with it, and I understood its rhythms.

Dreams are pure imaginative substance, and as such they're an amazing resource for writers, but you don't have to be asleep in order to enter the House of Dreams. Writing, like any other creative practice, can open the door, and anyone can go through.

The cost of entry is giving up the idea that the only point of dreaming and writing is as a way to increase your efficacy in the world. If you approach dreams purely as a source of information about waking life, and if you regard writing as a waste of time unless you are published, then you are fixed in this world, and will not enter the House of Dreams.

This is not to say that you should never seek information about waking life in dreams, or make a career from your writing, but simply that these are secondary aims. First, explore the whole territory, unencumbered by baggage from the day-to-day world.

Then, if you want to interpret, you can do so with confidence, because you will know when interpretation is appropriate, and how to avoid the pitfalls of confusion and misunderstanding. If you want to write for a living, you will be so closely connected to your inner world, that you will be less disheartened by the demands and difficulties of the modern market.

When you engage with the dream-world on its own terms, you have access to a much wider and deeper experience of yourself and the world. You are on a path to personal transformation.

You don't need to devote a lifetime to the dream-journey or become a professional author in order to have this experience, just as you don't need to be a Buddhist monk to feel the benefits of meditation.

Any daily practice will put you in the zone – a dream remembered, a scrap of dialogue overheard; a page of stream-of-consciousness writing; a sketch, a paragraph, a poem. The point is the process. The more you practise, with this focus, the more your life will be transformed.

The exploration may not be a path to happiness – in fact, at times, it may lead away from happiness, because happiness is an illusion. Happiness cannot exist without its Shadow side, unhappiness.

Dreaming and writing may take you into places which feel confusing and unsettling, but darkness is part of the human experience, so although inhabiting all the hidden places of the Self may not bring unalloyed happiness, it will bring feelings of personal empowerment and peace of mind.

It will bring authenticity and, out of truth, compassion, because truth is dark as well as light, uncertain as well as certain, uncontrollable as well as possible to master, and however much we may want to believe that we can fully comprehend it, nobody can.

This is surrender of the small self we think we are, to the larger Self that we actually are. It is surrender to life and, when we surrender, life will surge through in abundant inspirations and possibilities.

Dreams come through you, they are not of you. Like

your children, like your writing, they have their own soul and energy. At the moment of conception, you know that it will be a baby, a book, a painting, a dream remembered, but you don't know what it will be like.

The one certain thing is, it will change you; it will make demands of you, and you will have to find the resources in yourself to meet those demands, because you will have a duty of care to the new thing you have brought into the world. And so it is that the creation creates the creator; writing creates the writer, dreaming creates the dreamer.

Before the journey, we walk the same roads, and pass the gate in the hedge, day after day, never thinking to pause and look over. Consequently, our lives may feel narrow, confined, repetitive, vaguely unsatisfying.

'The forest of dreams was once a dark impenetrable place,
before the journey.'

As writers – even those who write professionally – we may suffer from anxiety, impatience and blocks in our creative process; we may become obsessed and distracted by the worldly stuff of promotions and sales figures, public appearances and prizes. We can lose sight of the whole reason why we do it, the joy of it, which is precisely that it isn't of this world; it's beyond the gate, beneath the water.

Whichever way you come to the inner world or House of Dreams, through dream-awareness or creative work, or any spiritual practice, it will change you. It will bend you to its rules and requirements; it will make you patient, open and receptive; it will demand of you both courage and persistence.

It will change the world of your everyday, bringing colour, movement, magic and possibilities; layers of meaning, stories and secrets. It will ground and energise your creativity, so that you can always write 'happily and with self-trust'.

That is the beauty of writing in the House of Dreams.

Related Reading

Arrien, Angeles *The Tarot Handbook: Practical Applications of Ancient Visual Symbols*
This is my favourite book on tarot; it refers to the Aleister Crowley Thoth tarot deck, and is very rich in detail.

Blake, William His poetry, paintings and prose are all wonderful to dip.

Brand, Paul; Yancey, Philip *Pain: The Gift Nobody Wants*
This thought-provoking book by a doctor and pain specialist discusses the purpose of pain.

Brande, Dorothea *Becoming a Writer*
First published in the 1930's and still in print, this book is a brilliant starting point for thinking about yourself as a writer.

Cameron, Julia *The Artist's Way: A Spiritual Path to Higher Creativity*
I particularly recommend this one for writers who feel stuck and want to get writing again.

Campbell, Joseph *The Hero with a Thousand Faces*
This book explores the hero's journey through myths and legends from different times and places.

Castaneda, Carlos *The Art of Dreaming*
I love this fascinating exploration into dreaming in a different culture.

Epel, Naomi *Writers Dreaming*
Naomi Epel interviews authors about how they use dreams in their writing process.

Friedman, Joe *The Dream Workbook*
This gives an excellent overview of the Western dream tradition.

Garfield, Patricia *Creative Dreaming*
Exciting and inspiring, this work on dreaming traditions from different cultures opened up new ways into dreaming for me.

Goldberg, Natalie *Writing down the Bones: Freeing the Writer Within*
This is one of my favourite books for writers - a kind of Tao of writing.

Hillman, James *The Dream and the Underworld*
James Hillman is my favourite dream writer – not easy to read, but well worth the effort. Another book I love by him is *The Soul's Code: In Search of Character and Calling*, which explores ideas about personal destiny and the 'acorn theory'.

Hughes, Ted *Poetry in the Making*
Originally a collection of radio talks, this little book is full of wonderful writing about writing.

Jung, Carl Gustav *Memories, Dreams, Reflections*
In this book, a great dreamer talks about his lifetime of dreaming.

King, Stephen *On Writing*
This is a mix of method and memoir from a master storyteller.

Maass, Donald *Writing the Breakout Novel*
If you're an author wanting to increase your audience,

Maass explains how to tap into the zeitgeist and create bestselling fiction.

Mallon, Brenda *The Illustrated Guide to Dreams: Dream Symbols and Their Meanings*
If you'd like to interpret your dreams, this is a clear introduction to dream interpretation from a very experienced therapist.

Martin, PW *Experiment in Depth: A Study of the Work of Jung, Eliot and Toynbee*
It's not a light read, but I like this thoughtful and inspiring exploration into soul.

McCabe, Mary Jo *Learn to See: An Approach to Your Inner Voice through Symbols*
This contains lots of practical exercises to help you become more aware of the symbolic layer of being.

McNiff, Shaun *Art as medicine: Creating a Therapy of the Imagination*
An art therapist explores creative work as soulful experience.

Mother Mary Agnes *For Love Alone*
Mother Mary-Agnes founded the religious community, the Society of Our Lady of the Isles; this is her story.

Pollack, Rachel *Seventy-Eight Degrees of Wisdom*, Books 1 & 2
Most people acknowledge this as the best introduction to tarot for beginners. It's based on the Rider-Waite pack.

Rilke, Rainer Maria *Letters to a Young Poet*
An author talks about the writing life.

Tolle, Eckhart *The Power of Now*
This explores the nature of time and spiritual reality.

Ueland, Brenda *If You Want to Write*
Ueland's great on the timeless topic of writing – another classic first published in the 1930's.

Upczak, Patricia Rose *Synchronicity, Signs and Symbols*
This is a short, easy read, though I don't personally like the glossary-of-meanings approach at the end.

Vogler, Christopher *The Writer's Journey*
When you've read this screenwriter's exploration of the hero's journey, you'll never look at blockbuster movies in the same way.

Zweig, Connie and Abrams, Jeremiah (editors) *Meeting the Shadow: The Hidden Power of the Dark Side of Human Nature*
This collection of essays by a wide range of authors is fascinating and thought provoking.

Permissions

Every effort has been made to trace the copyright holders of material quoted in this book. I am grateful to all the authors and publishers who have granted me permission to quote from these texts:

Private Myths: Dreams and Dreaming, by Anthony Stevens © 1995 Anthony Stevens. Reproduced by permission of the author c/o Rogers, Coleridge and White Ltd, 20 Powis Mews, London W11 1JN

If You Want to Write, by Brenda Ueland © 1938 Brenda Ueland (Martino Publishing)

Playing and Reality, by DW Winnicott, pp 65 and 69 © 1982 DW Winnicott (Routledge)

Learn to See: An Approach to Your Inner Voice Through Symbols, by Mary Jo McCabe, p 28 © 1994 Mary Jo McCabe (Blue Dolphin, Nevada City, CA)

Brief quotes from pp 13, 55 from *The Dream and the Underworld*, by James Hillman © 1979 James Hillman. Reprinted by permission of HarperCollins Publishers. Electronic rights granted by Klaus Ottman, Spring Publications

New Collected Poems, by Wendell Berry © 2012 Wendell Berry. Reprinted by permission of Counterpoint

Art as Medicine: Creating a Therapy of the Imagination, by Shaun McNiff © 1992 Shaun McNiff. Reprinted by arrangement with Shambhala Publications Inc, Boston, MA www.shambhala.com and Little Brown Book Group www.littlebrown.co.uk

Creative Dreaming by Patricia Garfield © 1974 Patricia Garfield

Writers Dreaming, by Naomi Epel (Vintage Books) Interview with Allan Gurganus © 1993 Allan Gurganus. Interview with Sue Grafton © 1993 Sue Grafton. Interview with Anne Rivers Siddons © 1993 Anne Rivers Siddons

Blackfoot Physics: A Journey into the Native American Universe, by F David Peat © by F David Peat (Fourth Estate)

The Dream Workbook, by Joe Friedman © 2007 Joe Friedman (Carroll and Brown)

Meeting Darkness on the Path, by William Carl Eichmann © 1990 William Carl Eichmann (first published in Gnosis Magazine)

Dictionary of Symbols, by Tom Chetwynd © 1982 Tom Chetwynd (Thorsons)

Acknowledgements

I would like to thank my generous readers Nicola Morgan, Lesley Howarth and Sian Morgan; Brenda Mallon, whose feedback on the dream sections I found really helpful, and Liz Kessler, who has encouraged me to keep going with this book ever since she read an early draft more than a decade ago.

Huge thanks also to my editor, Helen Greathead, to Becky Pickard, my designer, to Rachel Lawston who created the cover and to Sarah Mackie, my branding and marketing angel.

Finally, a happy wave hello to all my children and their partners, my ex-husband and my friends – wonderful companions on this life's journey.

About the Author

Since her first book was published in 1994, Jenny Alexander has written about 150 books for children and adults, articles in magazines including Mslexia, The Author and Junior Education, several interactive CDRoms and a writing app.

Jenny teaches workshops on the art and craft of writing fiction, non-fiction and memoir, for everyone from complete beginners to published authors. She has worked for national organisations such as The Arvon Foundation, The Society of Authors, The Scattered Authors' Society and The Writing Retreat, as well as a wide variety of local groups, from home-educated children to people in the workplace. Some of her workshops include creative dreaming and imagework.

Jenny's workshops taught me to stop panicking about my creativity and to start listening properly to my own inner thoughts. I've used her workshop ideas again and again to help me cope with creative problems.

Moira Butterfield
http://www.moirabutterfield.com/

During Jenny's collage workshop, which she led with a soulful gentleness, I had a sense that disparate parts of my mind spoke their sorrows and dreams, and discovered they all wanted the same things. Several years on, I am still nourished by the clarity and the freedom that emerged from the sweetness and excitement of that afternoon.

Moira Munro

http://www.moiramunro.com

I took part in one of Jen's dream workshops at a writing retreat. At first I was a little sceptical, but I was happy to give it a go. The exercise proved relaxing and enjoyable, and I thought that was the end of it. Then, ten minutes after it had finished, an answer to my plot problem seemed to come out of nowhere. Wow! The subconscious is amazing.

Paeony Lewis

http://paeonylewis.com

I am most grateful because in one short session she showed me the possibilities for taking my writing somewhere else, and now I am working on new ideas that expand what I learnt with her.

Alison Boyle

http://www.oxfordwriters.com/our-team.html

I often use Jenny's collage activity to explore the subconscious world of my stories. A great resource, and an inspiring writing teacher.

Lee Weatherly

www.usborne.com/angel

The story called 'Mow Top' in my ebook collection, 'Overheard in a Graveyard' sprang fully formed from one of Jenny's 'tear up magazines and make collages' exercises. I made the collage, couldn't think of anything to say about it, left it while I went to lunch. When I came back, the instant I saw it, the complete story leapt into my head.

Susan Price

http://www.susanpriceauthor.com/

I'm a great fan of Jenny's 'busting through blocks' collage workshops and have found them invaluable in unlocking the imagination and releasing creativity.

Celia Rees

http://www.celiarees.com

You can read more about Jenny's books and workshops on her website www.jennyalexander.co.uk

Final Word

I wrote this book for the same reason I teach workshops, because writing and dreaming have been great sources of joy and revelation to me throughout my life, and I love to share the good stuff.

If you have enjoyed reading it, or found something useful in its pages, please would you take a moment to share the good stuff too, by telling your friends or posting a short review on the website where you bought it?

Wishing you amazing dreams and happy writing!

Jenny Alexander

Happy Writing: Beat Your Blocks, Be Published and Find Your Flow

Every writer feels stuck sometimes, but you don't have to be beaten by writer's block. This guide offers insights and practical strategies to help you

- spot self-sabotaging thoughts and build your writing confidence
- create writing goals that feel meaningful and exciting
- understand all the stages of the creative process
- deal with technical problems such as plotting and pacing
- decide on your best route to publication

It will help you if you're stuck, but even if you aren't stuck, read it anyway, because knowing how to deal with problems should they arise is the best way of making sure they don't.

A lifeline to anyone who is stuck in their writing or suffering from any kind of block. Jenny Alexander speaks to all writers, whether they are just starting or have been writing for years.

Celia Rees, award-winning author

Get Writing!

Writing for 20 minutes a day is a tried and tested way of breaking through writer's block, and Jenny Alexander's app, *Get Writing!*, delivers a new writing task to your iPhone or iPad every day for 28 days.

What makes *Get Writing!* unique is that it's structured towards creating a finished piece in that 20 minutes a day. There are 4 stages, each consisting of 7 writing tasks:

Stage 1: Start writing
Stage 2: Fire up your imagination
Stage 3: Write a complete story
Stage 4: Redraft and make it better

So what are you waiting for? Download it from the Apple App Store and get writing!

30061439R00181

Printed in Poland
by Amazon Fulfillment
Poland Sp. z o.o., Wrocław